THE AUTHORS

# THE COMPLETE
# KANO JIU-JITSU

## (JUDO)

### BY

### H. IRVING HANCOCK
### and
### KATSUKUMA HIGASHI

DOVER PUBLICATIONS, INC.
NEW YORK

Published in Canada by General Publishing Company, Ltd., 30 Lesmill Road, Don Mills, Toronto, Ontario.

Published in the United Kingdom by Constable and Company, Ltd., 10 Orange Street, London WC 2.

This Dover edition, first published in 1961, is an unaltered republication of the work originally published by G. P. Putnam's Sons in 1905, except that the last two sections (26 pages) on serious and fatal blows and *kuatsu,* or the restoration of life, have been omitted, because their use to the public is doubtful and they do not affect the over-all value of the book.

*International Standard Book Number: 0-486-20639-4*
*Library of Congress Catalog Card Number: 61-1980*

Manufactured in the United States of America
Dover Publications, Inc.
180 Varick Street
New York, N.Y. 10014

# A FOREWORD BY
# H. IRVING HANCOCK

THIS is a far more ambitious and comprehensive attempt at a descriptive interpretation of the Japanese art of jiu-jitsu, or jiudo, than was undertaken in the writers' earlier volumes on the subject. Yet this larger and final volume on the subject was to be expected, and probably will be welcomed.

This volume, therefore, presents, in its entirety, the Kano system of jiu-jitsu, devised by Professor Jiguro Kano, with the additions thereto that have been made by those famous jiu-jitsians, Hoshino and Tsutsumi. Since the adoption of the Kano system in Japan as the official jiu-jitsu of the government in the army, navy, and police departments, the older and greatly inferior systems have begun to drop into disuse. The newer generation in Japan is devoting its attention wholly to the Kano methods.

This system begins with the simplest of combat tricks and progresses by degrees to tricks that may be made, in stress of dire necessity, most disastrous and even deadly. Yet it must not be inferred from this that the practice of jiu-jitsu is dangerous. Far from it ! The writer has in his desk at the moment of writing a manuscript copy of a report made to the War Department by Colonel Oliver E. Wood, U.S. military *attaché* at Tokio, in which the statement is made that, out of four thousand pupils who attended the Kano school, not one was permanently injured.

In friendly contests the more serious tricks of jiu-jitsu are not practised with any intention of causing harm.

Between Japanese students the tricks are practised lightly and swiftly, yet with care not to cause the injuries that would result from a severe application of the work.

Mr. Higashi has modestly understated my reasons for wishing to have his aid in the preparation of this volume. I desired to have him collaborate with me because he is one of the leading exponents of Kano jiu-jitsu. At the age of eighteen he was instructor in jiu-jitsu at Doshisha College, Kioto, Japan. He also coached the students in baseball, football and other sports, and was besides instructor in mathematics.

H. IRVING HANCOCK.

# PREFACE
# BY THE JAPANESE AUTHOR

IT is with a great deal of pleasure that I have joined Mr. Hancock in the preparation of this, the first complete and authentic work in any language that explains the highest school of *jiu-jitsu* as that art is taught and practised by the adepts of Japan.

Years ago Mr. Hancock was a familiar figure in the *jiu-jitsu* schools of Japan. He was always an admirer of our race, and has shown keen insight into many phases of our national life as we ourselves understand it. Of *jiu-jitsu* he became a zealous disciple, both on account of its value as a means of physical training and as a method of combat.

When he came to Japan Mr. Hancock was more than ordinarily well versed in the ways of *jiu-jitsu*, as he had learned much from Japanese in this country. In the schools of our country he finished what he had begun at home. While in actual combat work Mr. Hancock does not claim rank with our adepts, he is nevertheless highly skilful in the practice of the art, and his comprehension of the theory of *jiu-jitsu* exceeds, undoubtedly, that possessed by any other man not a native of Japan. After having studied the work of the many older and inferior schools, my collaborator applied himself to the thorough study of the most modern and effective school of the art, the Kano system, which is to-day the real *jiu-jitsu* of Japan, and which has been made official by its exclusive recognition by the Japanese government for purposes of instruction in our army and navy and in our police departments.

Mr. Hancock's earlier books on the subject were intended to pave the way, to prepare the Occidental public for this

# PREFACE BY THE JAPANESE AUTHOR

final and complete exposition of *jiu-jitsu* as it is taught by order of our government. As I have intimated, there are many systems of *jiu-jitsu* in Japan, but the others are all older and less effective than the modern, eclectic Kano method. These more ancient methods have become practically obsolete in Japan. It is our racial instinct to turn to the newest and best in everything. Japanese who have learned the old and now obsolete methods have found themselves compelled to forget their hard-acquired knowledge and to take instruction all over again in the more scientific Kano methods. An adept of the first rank in the older schools finds himself helpless before an ordinarily clever student of Kano.

The Kano system, at the time of its adoption by the Japanese government, consisted of forty-seven tricks of combat and fifteen "serious" tricks. Additions and amplifications have been made by those great teachers, Hoshino and Tsutsumi, until now the complete system, as we teach it, comprises one hundred and sixty tricks. These are divided into three sections. The first includes sixty tricks of combat in strict sequence. These tricks are intended as a preparation for the more advanced tricks of Section II. In the Second Section the pupil is taught how to apply advantages that he has gained by the tricks he already knows. More scientific tricks are imparted to him, and toward its close the Second Section verges on the "serious" work of *jiu-jitsu*.

In the preparation of a work of such magnitude Mr. Hancock naturally preferred to collaborate with a native Japanese professor of the art. He has been unremitting in his efforts to have Occidentals taught *jiu-jitsu* properly at the outset, by ignoring the lesser and obsolete schools of the art and acquiring only the Kano system that is official in Japan. Some Japanese have been engaged in this country in teaching the work of the lesser schools. Through Mr. Hancock's praiseworthy and consistent

# PREFACE BY THE JAPANESE AUTHOR

efforts to have only the Kano system taught to Americans we have been associated in its introduction in this country. It was natural, therefore, that Mr. Hancock should turn to myself for collaboration. We have laboured long and arduously to make this work so exhaustive that it shall have no detail lacking. We present this work to the public with confidence that no apology is needed for the length and the multiplicity of detail inseparable from the complete exposition of every phase of the Kano system of *jiu-jitsu*.

In these pages will be found all the parts of the work as it is now being taught by a Japanese *confrère* of mine to the midshipmen at the U. S. Naval Academy at Annapolis. Some confusion has arisen over the employment of the term "jiudo." To make the matter clear I will state that *jiudo* is the term selected by Professor Kano as describing his system more accurately than *jiu-jitsu* does. Professor Kano is one of the leading educators of Japan, and it is natural that he should cast about for the technical word that would most accurately describe his system. But the Japanese people generally still cling to the more popular nomenclature and call it *jiu-jitsu*.

*Jiu-jitsu*, or *jiudo*, is in Japan the art of the gentleman. It is not surprising, therefore, that the highest evolution of our ancient Japanese style of combat should come about in these days through the efforts of Professor Jiguro Kano. To him we owe much, and also to Messrs. Hoshino and Tsutsumi, who, by their toil, have rounded out the Kano system to its present perfection and supremacy.

KATSUKUMA HIGASHI.

42 WEST 65TH STREET,
  NEW YORK, March 10, 1905.

# RULES GOVERNING *JIU-JITSU* CONTESTS IN JAPAN

*Translated from the Japanese by Katsukuma Higashi.*

(1)   Each contestant shall wear coat and belt.

(2)   A contestant shall be deemed to have been defeated when his two shoulders and hips shall have touched the floor, provided that said contestant shall have reached this position on the floor through having been thrown down.   (See modification in Rule 8.)

(3)   A contestant shall be deemed to have been defeated when in such position on the floor, if said combatant cannot free himself from his opponent's arms within two seconds' time.

(4)   A contestant shall be deemed to have been defeated when from any cause or causes he may become unconscious.   But it is not permitted to use serious tricks when the wrestling bout is between friends.   Such tricks as kicking and the breaking of arms, legs, or neck are barred.

(5)   A combatant shall be deemed to have been defeated when he has been reduced to submission through the employment by his opponent of any hold or trick.

(6)   When a defeated combatant finds himself obliged to acknowledge his submission, he must pat or hit the floor or his antagonist's body, or somewhere, with his hand or foot.   This patting with foot or hand is to be regarded as a token of surrender.

(7)   When a defeated combatant pats or hits the floor, or anywhere, in token of submission, the victor must at once let go his hold.

(8)   When a combatant shall have allowed his shoulders

and hips to have touched the floor, but shall have done so with the intention of thereby throwing his opponent, the combatant who has so allowed his shoulders and hips to touch the floor shall not be deemed to have been defeated.

(9) When wrestling on a mat or mattress, it is permissible for a contestant who is on the defensive to fall in any way that he pleases; but for defensive purposes it is generally better to lie upon the back.

(10) When a combatant lying on his back for defensive purposes shall be raised and downed again by his opponent, and made once more to touch shoulders and hips to the floor, the combatant who has been so raised and downed shall be deemed to have been defeated, but not otherwise.

When one not a jiu-jitsian is matched against a jiu-jitsian, it is necessary that the former, in addition to comprehending the foregoing rules, should be informed of the following rules:

(1) It is understood and agreed that the *jiu-jitsu* man, whether he fights a boxer or contests with a wrestler, shall be allowed to use in his defence any of the tricks that belong to the art of *jiu-jitsu*.

(2) It is further understood and agreed that the *jiu-jitsu* man assumes no responsibility for any injury or injuries caused by any act or thing done during the contest, and that the *jiu-jitsu* man shall be held free and blameless for any such ill effect or injury that may be received during the contest.

(3) Two competent witnesses representing each side, or four in all, shall see to it that these articles of agreement are properly drawn, signed, and witnessed, to the end that neither contestant or other participant in the match shall have cause for action on any ground or grounds resulting from any injury or injuries, or death, caused during the contest.

# HOW TO STUDY *JIU-JITSU*

In this volume all of the tricks of the Kano system are given strictly in their sequence. The student is advised that the only way in which to learn the work is to take up each trick in its order, and to master that trick thoroughly before passing on to another. In no other way can an effective knowledge of *jiu-jitsu* be obtained.

In the first place, the few feats of falling, which precede the actual work of combat, should be patiently mastered, and the reasons back of each step should be perfectly understood. Mastery of this preliminary work will make the learning of the combat tricks possible and easy.

A good deal has been accomplished when the student has fully mastered the work that is laid down in the First Section. He should not be in haste to pass on to the Second Section, nor from the Second to the Third.

If the reader finds that he fumbles in a certain phase of a given trick, he is advised to keep practising at that trick until he is positive of his mastery of it.

# CONTENTS

# KANO JIU=JITSU

## SECTION I

# Kano Jiu-Jitsu

No. 1.  Trick 1.  Phase 1

First of all it is of great importance that the pupil should learn to fall correctly.  Skill in this seemingly simple art of throwing himself just right will save the pupil from many injuries, and make his work easier, as he goes on in the practice of the art.  Illustration No. 1 shows the standing position for the start in falling.

### Trick 1.    Phase 2

Fall lightly on the palms, with thumbs and fingers pointing *invariably* forward. Falling with the hands so placed prevents sprains or fractures of the arms. In this fall the left foot should go well back, while the right foot takes a long step forward. The weight of the body is supported, for the most part, on the toes of the right foot, as is shown in illustration No. 2.

### Trick 1.    Phase 3

Quickly bring back the right foot to a position beside the left. Practise strongly sustaining the weight of the body on the toes and palms.

No. 2. Trick 1. Phase 2

No. 3. Trick 1. Phase 3

Trick 1.  Phase 4

Raise your back as high as possible, then lower it again, and repeat as long as this exercise can be continued without strain. Illustration No. 4 shows the back at its highest elevation.

Trick 1.  Phase 5

Lower the body, as shown in illustration, until it rests on the chest only.  No other portion of the trunk may touch the floor, and the feet may touch only at the toes.  Do not let the knees touch the floor.

No. 4.   Trick 1.   Phase 4

No. 5.   Trick 1.   Phase 5

### Trick 2.  Phase 1

Take the starting point as directed in Phase 4 of Trick 1.  Fall quickly to the right (or left) side in such way that the shoulder cannot be made to touch the ground.  Illustration No. 6 shows the method of falling to the right.

### Trick 2.  Phase 2

Practise falling to the left, as depicted in illustration No. 7.

Note.—No student of *jiu-jitsu* should neglect repeated and earnest practice in the two foregoing tricks.  Always in landing on the palms, make sure that the fingers and thumbs point forward.  Falling upon the hands with fingers and thumbs pointing sideways, or to the rear, involves the risk of breaking wrists, elbows, or shoulders.

# Kano Jiu-Jitsu

No. 6.  Trick 2.  Phase 1

No. 7.  Trick 2.  Phase 2

No. 8. Trick 3. Phase 2

Phase 1 is the same as in Trick 1, Phase 1.

Phase 2.   Practise this slowly at first, but with increasing rapidity as time goes on.   Resting the weight of the body on the left leg, advance the right leg well forward, and come down to squatting position, holding your arms well forward, as if trying to throw an adversary over a shoulder or at either side of the body.   Then reverse the practice by starting with all the weight borne on the right leg and sending the left leg forward as you come down to the squat. Next practise the same feat by starting with the weight of the body resting on the toes of one foot.   The heel of that foot must not touch the floor until the squatting position has been reached, as shown in illustration No. 8.   This work must be mastered thoroughly by the beginner, or many of the throws described in the illustrations and text to follow cannot be made with certainty.

No. 9. Trick 4. Phase 1

Standing ready to fall, as when thrown by an adversary. Illustration No. 9 shows the right leg to be well forward, and the body held in an easy position.

No. 10. Trick 4. Phase 2

Turn to the side on which you are to fall. Lean well forward on the leg of the side to which you are to fall. Study the position as shown in illustration No. 10. It is highly important that, at the very outset of this fall, the head be depressed well against the chest, and turned to the opposite side from that on which you are to fall.

**No. 11. Trick 4. Phase 3**

In continuation throw a somersault backward so that neither the head nor the point of the shoulder touch the ground. Land, instead, on the shoulder-blade. See illustration No. 11.

**No. 12. Trick 4. Phase 4**

In instant continuation of the somersault come up to the position shown in the illustration above. Rest on the knee of the side to which you fall. The other knee is to be slightly extended, as shown. The relative position of the knees must never be varied. The position at recovery that is shown in illustration No. 12 is to be gained with exactness.

No. 13. Trick 5. Phase 1

Take the position shown in illustration No. 13, with your left hand at your opponent's elbow; your right hand seizes him at his upper left arm.

**No. 14.  Trick 5.  Phase 2**

Swiftly change the hold with your left hand to one under opponent's elbow, push his elbow up, and drag his arm toward you.  This forces your opponent to advance his right foot.  Just at the instant before this foot of his touches the floor kick his ankle at the outside and throw him.  See illustration No. 14.

**No. 15.  Trick 6.  Phase 1**

When your opponent seizes you at the under sides of the upper
arms make a quick change so as to seize him under his upper arms.
See illustration No. 15.

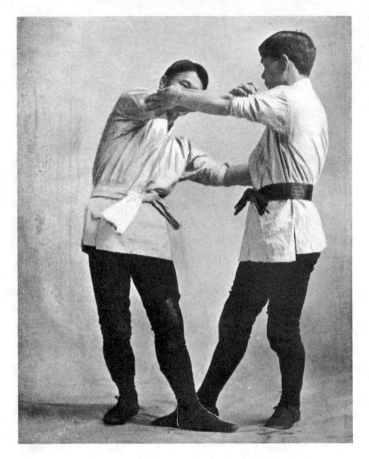

**No. 16. Trick 6. Phase 2**

In the preceding phase the assailant's left foot was forward. The assailant now quickly steps his left foot backward, at the same time yanking his victim's left arm toward him. This forces victim to throw his left foot inside of his assailant's right foot, and the assailant now kicks the exposed ankle, as shown in illustration No. 16, and makes a throw as in preceding trick.

**No. 17. Trick 7. Phase 2**

Phase 1. Stand at the position shown in Phase 1 of Trick 6.

Phase 2. Move across the floor sideways. Your opponent, in order to keep his balance, is obliged to move his feet with yours. For instance, if you are forcing your adversary to move to his own right, watch until he has moved his right foot and is about to follow it with his left. Just before his left foot can touch the floor kick it at the ankle from the outside with your right foot, thus forcing his two feet together, as shown in illustration No. 17. Instantly, before your opponent has time to move his feet apart, throw him over your extended right foot.

[19]

**No. 20.  Trick 9.  Phase 2**

Move your right leg, with a wide sweep, around to the left of your opponent, seeking opportunity to bring your right knee with smart forceful impact against the outside of his left knee, making it impossible for the adversary to move his left foot quickly.   Now, by the control that you have over his body by means of your hold on his right arm and at the left edge of his coat, throw your opponent over your right knee to the ground.

**No. 21.  Trick 10.  Phase 1**

Give your adversary a chance to seize you at your shoulder.  As he does so slip your thumb inside his coat sleeve and take the firmest hold possible.  (If he wears regulation street coat the hold can be taken as well as on a coat with sleeve of elbow length.)  It makes no difference where you seize him with your other hand.  Study illustration No. 21.

**No. 22. Trick 10. Phase 2**

When in the position described in the preceding phase, let go of your adversary with your right hand. Pass this right hand, open, swiftly up before his face in order to confuse him. At the same instant raise your right foot *high* and pass it by his right thigh, your right foot landing on the ground well behind your opponent. Now, swiftly turn your back to your opponent, bringing his captured right arm under your right shoulder. Still retaining the original hold with your left hand, use your right hand to seize his right wrist. Bending well forward, as shown in illustration No. 22, straighten your left knee with strong pressure against the outside of your antagonist's right knee.

[24]

# Kano Jiu-Jitsu

No. 23.   Trick 10.   Phase 3

Lowering your own body still more, push your left knee against your antagonist's right knee, as shown in illustration No. 23, pull hard on his right arm and force him to turn a somersault over your right shoulder to the ground.

## Trick 10.   Phase 4

As your victim falls, swing your own body so as to fall with him in position shown.   Pull his captured arm as far around you as you can, pressing your upper right arm forcibly against the right side of his neck.   When necessary, the pressure that is shown in illustration No. 24 may be used for strangling an opponent.

## Trick 11.   Phase 2

Phase 1.   The position is the same as in Phase 4, Trick 10.

Phase 2.   This involves a form of " submission " on the part of the victim.   Change your own position so that your right arm is under the victim's right arm just above the elbow.   Use your own right knee under your right elbow for leverage power.   Seize your victim's right wrist with your left hand, and thus bend his right arm back the " wrong way," as if to break it.   The pain forces the victim to submit before serious consequences follow this pressure upon the arm.

No. 24. Trick 10. Phase 4

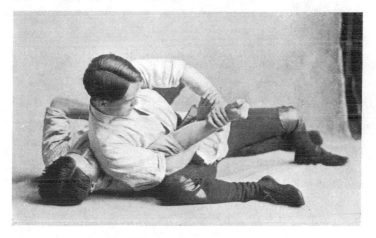

No. 25. Trick 11. Phase 2

**No. 26. Trick 12. Phase 1**

The assailant, with his right hand, seizes the front or edge of his adversary's coat. The latter protects himself by seizing the assailant's right wrist with his left hand, at the same time stepping well back on the left foot. Should the assailant make a seizure with his left hand, the man on the defensive guards himself by seizing that attacking left arm.

**No. 27.  Trick 12.  Phase 2**

Seize your opponent's right sleeve as shown, and bring your left foot past the outside of his right foot.

**No. 28. Trick 12. Phase 3**

Swing around so as to present your back to your opponent. At the same instant seize his right wrist with your left hand, and pull his captured arm strongly over your right shoulder. Pulling at your adversary's right arm as strongly as you can, thrust your haunch back forcibly against your opponent's kidney. At the same time, with the back of your left leg, hit the outside of his right knee, depriving him of his balance, and throwing him.

**No. 29. Trick 12. Phase 4**

If you are unable to throw your adversary over your shoulder while standing, sink quickly to right knee and extend the left leg, as shown in illustration No. 29. Now the throw can be easily made.

### Trick 12. Phase 5

When the victim is thrown from a standing position it is easy to land him on both shoulder blades. But, when thrown from a kneeling position, as in Phase 4, the victim may land on but one shoulder. Therefore it is highly important to retain the hold on his captured arm. Now, having thrown your victim, it will be necessary to use Trick 13.

### Trick 13. Phase 1

Bring up your right leg so that the knee is under the victim's upper arm at the back. Retaining your hold at your adversary's wrist with your left hand, bend his captured arm backward over your knee as if to break it. At the same time press your thumb severely against the nerve at the upper end of the jaw-bone and under the lobe of his right ear, while the fingers of your same hand are employed in choking him.

No. 30.   Trick 12.   Phase 5

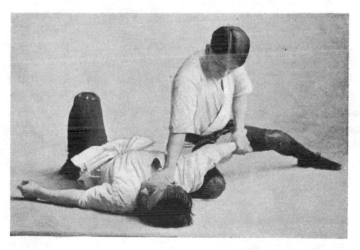

No. 31.   Trick 13.   Phase 1

No. 32.  Trick 14.  Phase 1

When your victim is held, as in foregoing trick, if he be very clever, he will succeed in getting a hold with his left hand at your right shoulder.  In this case take a strong hold against his left arm with your right.  Now, spring fairly over your victim's body, landing at his left, and, at the moment of making the spring, thrust your left arm under his neck and hold tightly.  The victim may now be held helpless for twenty seconds, and then counted out.

No. 33.  Trick 15.  Phase 1

When an adversary seizes you by the coat lapel, or the edge of
coat, first take off his hand.  This is accomplished by forcing the
ball of your thumb under the ball of his thumb, while with your
second finger you press hard against the base of his thumb at the
back.  Force his thumb back, and he will be obliged to release his
hold.  As he does so, seize his wrist.

# Kano Jiu-Jitsu

**No. 34.  Trick 15.  Phase 2**

Swing to your victim's left side.  If he attempts to pull away his left arm, hold tightly with your left hand, and throw your hooked right arm forcibly back of his left elbow.  Now, swing still more to your left, pressing your haunch in the victim's left side and the back of your right knee strongly against the front of his left knee.  At the moment of making this swing carry his captured arm over your right shoulder, keeping the palm side of his fist uppermost.

[36]

# Kano Jiu-Jitsu

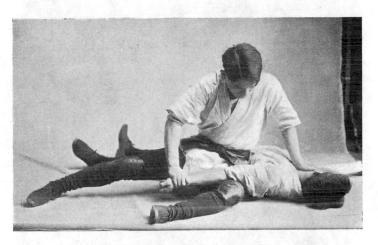

## No. 35.   Trick 15.   Phase 3

Make the throw over your shoulder, bringing the victim to the position shown above.   In this, as in all other throws over the shoulder, *remember to retain your hold on your victim's captured wrist!*  When you have brought your victim to the position shown in illustration No. 35, do not fall at his right side, as in this case you may give him an opening to free himself.   Instead, fall so as to sit upon him at his left side.   Bring up your left knee under the back of his upper left arm.   Force his arm backward as if attempting to break it, at the same time pushing upward with your left knee to assist in the torment.   Your left hand is pressed against the left side of his face so as to push his head over to the right.   If you prefer, you can employ your own right hand against his jawbone and throat, as in Trick 13.

**No. 36. Trick 16. Phase 1**

Give your opponent an opening to throw his right arm around your waist. As he does so, with your left hand seize his right upper arm at the back. Throw your right arm around your adversary's waist, seizing him at the belt over the left kidney.

**No. 37. Trick 16. Phase 2**

Pull hard with your right hand on your adversary's belt. This forces him to swing around and to step forward. As he does so, step forward quickly with your right foot. Lift this right foot *up high* so as to pass it outside his right thigh. Let your right foot land behind your opponent. Press your back against the victim's back. Bend forward, and, retaining the initial hold with your hands, you are ready for the throw.

**No. 38. Trick 16. Phase 3**

If you slip, the throw cannot be made. Bend, keeping your opponent's side on your back; then swing strongly to the left and make the throw.

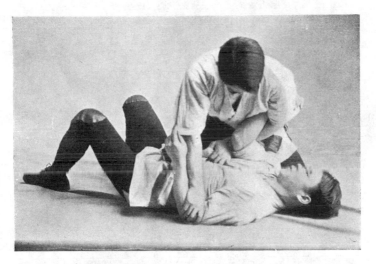

**No. 39. Trick 17. Phase 1**

In the preceding trick, when you throw your victim, your left hand is at his right upper arm. As you throw him, fall so that your left knee presses in his neck, while your right knee presses firmly against his right kidney. Force your left arm under his right elbow, and with your left hand seize his coat. With this hold it is easy to twist his right elbow. Bending forward, thus throw more pressure against his right arm and break it, if necessary. Your right hand holds your opponent's left elbow down.

**No. 40. Trick 18. Phase 1**

Here the opponents make an even start, for each has the same hold that the other has.

No. 41. Trick 18. Phase 2

Shift your hand to an under-arm hold on your opponent's right arm, and yank that arm toward you. At the same time take a wide side step to your left. While drawing your adversary's right arm toward you, change your hold on his left arm to an under-arm hold. At this moment of pulling his right arm toward you throw his left elbow well up. Lift your right foot *high,* pass it by his right thigh, and, as your right foot touches the ground, turn your back to your victim. Your haunch should be pressing in his right side, and both his arms are over your right shoulder.

No. 42   Trick 18.   Phase 3

In making the throw it is highly important to bend the right knee and to hold the left leg almost rigidly straight.   At the same time pull as hard as you can on your victim's left arm, and thus the throw is made.

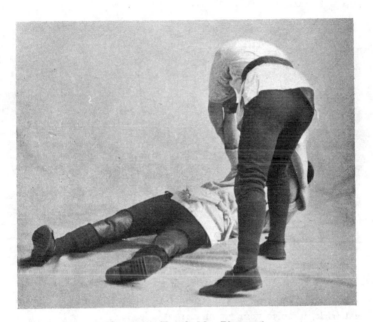

**No. 43.   Trick 18.   Phase 4**

When you have made the throw you should be holding your
opponent in just the same grips that you took before making the
throw.   In order to complete your victory it may now be necessary
to employ Trick 19.

**No. 44. Trick 19. Phase 1**

When you have secured the position described in Phase 4 of the last trick, jump to your victim's right side, keeping his right hand between your legs. His elbow is thus in position to be bent over your right leg. Throw yourself over on your back and continue the pressure on his right arm until the pain forces him to surrender.

No. 45.   Trick 20.   Phase 1

Here the combatant who wears the white belt has an excellent initial chance.   His right hand has taken hold inside the adversary's sleeve, his left hand has taken an under-arm hold.   The opponent in the black belt seizes both of his adversary's coat lapels.

**No. 46. Trick 20. Phase 2**

The man in the black belt pushes his adversary back with his hands. Then he pulls him toward him once more, and places a foot against the victim's stomach.

**No. 47.   Trick 20.   Phase 3**

Here the man who wears the black belt pulls his victim's shoulders toward him, at the same time pushing the other's body away with his foot; and the assailant falls over backward, landing on his shoulder-blades.  The victim is thrown over the assailant's head. Trick 21 is then used in sequence.

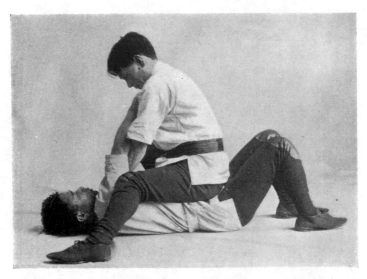

**No. 48.   Trick 21.   Phase 1**

The victim of the preceding trick lands on his back.   The assailant
sits upon him and seizes the victim's lapels.   Should the victim
secure a similar hold, the assailant twists his own arms outward
against the victim's arms.   Thus the victim's hold is broken.   In
securing his own lapel hold it is highly important that the assailant
seize the victim's left lapel fairly well up and the right lapel fairly
well down.   Now, force the left lapel severely to the right across
the victim's throat, and pull downward and to victim's left with the
right lapel.   Thus an effective choke may be administered.

No. 49.  Trick 22.  Phase 1

When an opponent seizes you at the upper arm, retaliate by thrusting your thumb inside his sleeve and wrapping your fingers in the cloth.  Take the firmest hold possible in this manner.

**No. 50.  Trick 22.  Phase 2**

When you have your opponent's left arm thus seized, throw off the hold of his right hand. (This throwing-off is a most valuable trick, and may be accomplished in either of two ways. When you desire to throw off an adversary's clutch, release your own hand that grasps his same arm. Then, with your fist under his " funny bone," hit that bone a severe blow. Or, release your own hand, and strike the inside of his forearm severely with your elbow. Both of these methods should be practised repeatedly.) Bend forward, yanking your adversary's right arm across the back of your neck, and thrust your right arm back of his right knee.

No. 51.  Trick 22.  Phase 3

Bend still farther forward, pull strongly on your intended victim's left arm, and yank his right knee up.

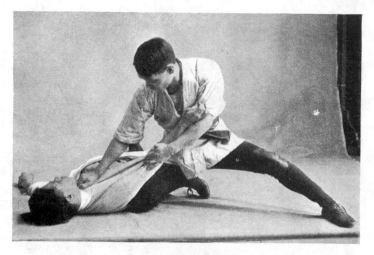

**No. 52. Trick 22. Phase 4**

Throw your victim to the position shown in illustration. Thrust your right knee forcibly under his right shoulder. Seize his collar and push it against your victim's throat. Employ Trick 13.

**No. 53. Trick 23. Phase 1**

When an opponent attacks you at your right side, throw your right arm around his neck, and seize his right elbow with your left hand.

**No. 54. Trick 23. Phase 2**

Pull your opponent's right arm forcibly toward you, at the same time wrapping your right leg around his left leg, as shown in illustration No. 54.

[56]

No. 55. Trick 23. Phase 3

Suddenly abandon the foregoing feint and place your feet in front of your opponent's, with the backs of your knees pressing against the fronts of his knees. Your left hip should press against your opponent's right kidney.

**No. 56. Trick 23. Phase 4**

Bending well forward with your right arm over your victim's neck, throw him over your back. If necessary, lift your opponent's left knee with your left hand.

No. 57.  Trick 24.  Phase 2

Phase 1.  Take the same hold as in Trick 23, Phase 2.

Phase 2.  (No illustration.)  When you throw your right arm around your opponent's neck, seize his right elbow with your left hand.  This leaves him no hold except to seize you around the waist with both arms.  Now, suddenly change your right arm so that it is around your adversary's neck from in front, thus forcing his head backward.  At the same time press your right knee against the back of his left knee, and fall backward.  This causes your victim also to fall backward, and, as he falls, with your right arm you can administer severe, dazing choking.

## Trick 25

**Phase 1.** The same hold is taken as is described in Phase 2 of Trick 23.

**Phase 2.** (No illustration.) With your right arm still around your victim's neck, and your right foot still wrapped around his left lower leg seize your own right wrist with your left hand. Pull your right forearm strongly toward your shoulder, thus severely crushing your adversary's jaw between your right shoulder and your right forearm, as if you held his jaw in a strong vise. This crushing of the jaw is a terrible punishment. As soon as you have begun the crushing of your adversary's jaw, throw yourself forward on your knees, carrying him down with you. Continue the jaw-crushing pressure until your opponent surrenders.

No. 58.   Trick 26.   Phase 2

Phase 1.   (No illustration.)   Your opponent has seized you with his right hand at your left upper arm, and his left hand at your right elbow.

Phase 2.   Pull your assailant's right arm toward you, at the same time stepping well back on your left foot.   This forces your assailant to advance his right foot.   Now, release your right-hand hold on his left arm and press your right hand against his right shoulder.   At the same instant kick the back of your adversary's right knee with the back of your own right calf.   While doing so pull at his right arm, push at his right shoulder, and thus throw him over backward.

**No. 59. Trick 27. Phase 1**

When your opponent has seized you at your upper arm, take an elbow-hold as shown in illustration No. 59. Release your right arm by one of the throw-offs already described. All that follows is done almost simultaneously. With your left hand pull your opponent's right arm toward you. With your right hand seize his left shoulder and push against it. Your adversary, when his right arm is pulled, will advance his right foot. Thrust your own right leg forward and past the outside of his at the knee. Sink to your left knee. Throw your opponent over your extended right leg.

No. 60.   Trick 28.   Phase 1

When your opponent wishes to throw you to his own left side, he feints as if intending to throw you to his right.   As he does so, hook your right foot back of his right ankle, which will prevent him from lifting and placing his right foot in such manner that he can make the throw.

**No. 61.   Trick 28.   Phase 2**

Follow up this advantage by releasing your right arm by means of a throw-off.   With your right hand seize your adversary at his right shoulder.   With your left hand pull his right arm forcibly toward you, and throw your right leg back of his as if to kick it from under him.   But this is only a feint—" teasing."

No. 62.  Trick 28.  Phase 3

Again pull your adversary's right arm toward you with your left
hand, and with your right hand again push at his right shoulder.
At the same time fall upon your left knee, and extend your right leg,
which must be rigid, past the outside of his right leg, just below
his knee.  Now, throw your opponent over to his right.

**No. 63.  Trick 29.  Phase 1**

When you have thrown your victim, by means of the preceding trick, retain the hold with which you threw him.  With your left hand, that has the hold at his elbow, push his elbow severely as if trying to force his arm to " bend the wrong way."  With the right hand, that has a hold at your adversary's right shoulder, press against his jugular vein, in order to strangle him.

**No. 64.  Trick 29.  Phase 2**

Now force your right knee under your victim's right shoulder. Here one form of strangle-hold is employed.  Insert your right hand under the victim's coat-collar as far around to the left as you can secure the hold.  Pass your left arm under your right arm and seize the victim's right coat collar.  It is highly important that, in securing this hold, the backs of your hands be toward the victim and your palms toward yourself.  Now, retaining the hold, draw the hands closer together in order to effect the strangulation.  In this strangle-hold your muscular strength must be applied from the elbows.

**No. 65. Trick 30. Phase 1**

You have thrown off your opponent's hold on one side, as explained in Trick 22. At the moment of taking the hold, your left foot was forward. Now, step your left foot well backward. *Do not straighten the arm that has hold at your adversary's lapel! If you do, your adversary will have a chance to break your arm!* So, let your attacking arm remain bent, as shown in illustration No. 65.

No. 66. Trick 30. Phase 2

Swing your body slightly, and bring your left foot just outside your opponent's left foot. This leads your opponent to believe that you intend to throw him to his left. It gives him also an opportunity to throw you to your right. But instantly, before your victim can take advantage of this opening, swing your body again so that you thrust your extended, rigid right leg past the outside of his right leg, and, in the same swift movement, drop to your left knee.

[69]

**No. 67. Trick 30. Phase 3**

Bending well forward, throw the weight of your body on your left knee. Your right hand is already at your adversary's coat lapel. With your left hand seize the right edge of his coat below the lapel. Throw your victim over your right shoulder.

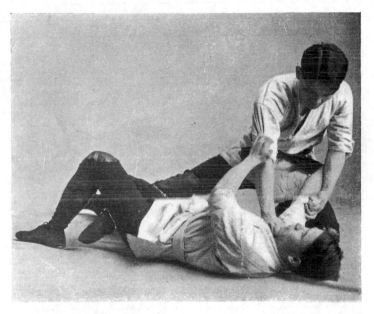

No. 68. Trick 30. Phase 4

In this case, as in all other cases where you make a throw, be careful not to lose the hold that you had at the moment of making the
throw.  Your left knee is close to your victim's head.  Your right
leg, still extended, is under your victim's right leg.  Hold his captured right arm strongly over your left upper leg.  With your right
hand grip tightly at the lapel, ready for the employment of the next
trick.

**No. 69. Trick 31. Phase 1**

This is another strangle-hold. Take it exactly as shown in illustration No. 69. If your elbows are bent your victim has a chance to knock your elbows up and to save himself from much of the strangulation. Note how the arms are held in the illustration. They are bent but little, and your left elbow is close to your left side. The second knuckle of the second finger of your right hand protrudes in advance of the other knuckles, and is pressed into the victim's right jugular. Your left hand, just below your right hand, seizes the victim's left lapel and pulls it strongly over toward his right shoulder. This completes the strangulation.

No. 70. Trick 32. Phase 1

Your opponent has seized you, and brings his right foot forward inside your right foot. His left hand has an under-hand hold on your right arm. Shift your right hand so that you have an under-hand hold on his left arm.

**No. 71.   Trick 32.   Phase 2**

Side-step with your left foot.   This forces the adversary to bring
his left foot forward and outside your right foot, as, if he did not do
this, he would be in a position to be thrown quickly.   As your victim
brings his left foot forward, use your right foot to step firmly on his
left toes.   At the same time use your right hand to push against his
neck.

**No. 72.   Trick 32.   Phase 3**

Of course your victim will try to pull away his captured foot, and
he may succeed.   So, to forestall him, raise your right foot and with
your right calf quickly kick the outside of his right leg.   In the same
instant raise your right hand from his neck and strike him a smart,
forceful blow at the side of his head, thus sending him to the ground
over your right leg.

**No. 73.   Trick 33.   Phase 1**

It must be borne in mind that a crafty *jiu-jitsian* always seems
to give his opponent splendid opportunities.  In this instance you
have given your adversary a chance to seize you at the belt.  Grab
his right upper arm, as shown in illustration No. 73.  Here your
right leg is forward.

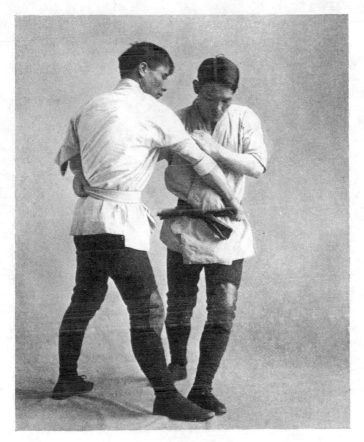

No. 74. Trick 33. Phase 2

Step well back on your right foot, and this gives you an opportunity to throw your right arm around your opponent's waist, seizing him at the belt.

**No. 75. Trick 33. Phase 3**

Bring your left foot close to your opponent's right, bending your left leg slightly. Pull hard on his right sleeve. Throw your right leg outside his right leg, in order to hold his right knee wedged, as shown in illustration No. 75.

**No. 76. Trick 33. Phase 4**

With your right leg placed as in the last phase, pull up hard on your adversary's belt with your right hand; with your left hand pull his right arm forcibly around toward you, and with your right foot kick his right leg from under him, and thus make the throw.

**No. 77. Trick 34. Phase 1**

Here both contestants are feinting—"fooling," the Japanese call it. Each is watching for an opportunity. Your opponent's right hand has seized your upper arm, and you have caught him at the elbow. The hold on the other side is unimportant. Bring your right leg outside your opponent's left, on which he is bearing his weight.

[80]

**No. 78. Trick 34. Phase 2**

In order to save himself your opponent has brought his right foot forward. At just the instant that he does this, swing your left leg around outside his right leg, so that your left knee is pressing against his right knee. And, in the same instant, shift your left hand to a hold at the back on his right shoulder. Make the throw by swinging your opponent forcibly over your left knee. In doing this you will aid yourself by swinging your own body around considerably.

**No. 79.   Trick 35.   Phase 1**

Your opponent has closed with you, and has thrust one thigh back of your thigh to throw you over backward.   Frustrate this attack by stepping quickly outside your adversary.   Thrust your right hand under his crotch, seizing the cloth at the back of the crotch.   Your left hand flies over to his left shoulder.

[82]

No. 80.  Trick 35.  Phase 2

With the leverage afforded by your hand at his crotch, push hard with your left hand at his left shoulder, and throw him over your knees, as shown in illustration No. 80.

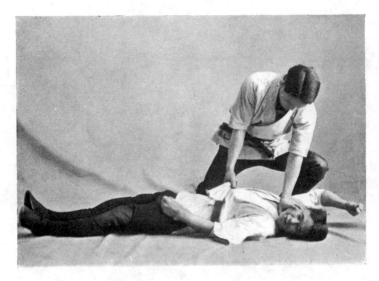

**No. 81.  Trick 35.  Phase 3**

As your victim falls, bring him to submission by falling with your left knee on his right arm, pulling up at his belt with your right hand, and using your left hand so that the tip of your second finger presses against the nerve under the lobe of his right ear, while your thumb digs against his jugular vein.

No. 82. Trick 36. Phase 1

Note the position that has been taken here, as shown in illustration No. 82.

**No. 83.   Trick 36.   Phase 2**

Release your hold around your adversary's waist.  With your
left hand gripping his right wrist, yank that wrist to your left side.
Your right hand must seize his right upper arm at the back.

**No. 84.  Trick 36.  Phase 3**

Now, quickly swing around, so as to fall upon your right knee, extending your left leg, held rigid, in front of your antagonist's left leg.  With severe pressure upon his right arm—this pressure is gained through the hold that you have just taken on the victim's captured right arm—fall over backward.  This trick, when applied with much force, will break your opponent's arm.  It is highly important to devote much practice to this trick, and always to remember it in the hour of need.

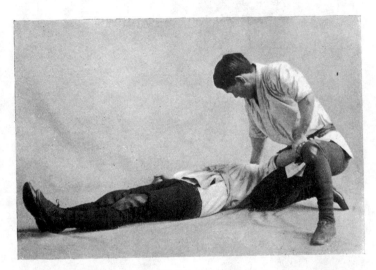

**No. 85.  Trick 37.  Phase 1**

When you have thrown your opponent by means of Trick 36, an opportunity will present itself to use this trick.  Your right knee is at your victim's left side.  Bend his left arm backward over your right leg, holding his left wrist with your left hand.  Push the palm of your right hand against the left side of your victim's face, thus forcing and holding his head away from you.  The arm-breaking pressure on your adversary's left arm will force him to surrender.

No. 86.  Trick 38.  Phase 1

When your opponent secures a chancery hold, as shown in illustration No. 86, throw your right arm around his waist, gripping at his belt or coat in the rear.  With your left hand seize his right wrist. Protect yourself from a choking by depressing your chin as much as possible upon your chest and making the neck muscles as tense as you can.

**No. 87.  Trick 38.  Phase 2**

The assailant's right wrist has been secured and held at just the
point where the wrist and the back-of-the-hand bones join.   Retain
both holds secured with your hands.   Dart your right leg between
your opponent's two legs.   Use your left leg to press against his right
leg, as shown in illustration No. 87.   Now throw yourself over backward.   As soon as you have fallen half-way backward—in other
words, as soon as you have gotten your opponent off his balance,
and have started him to going over with you—release the hold at his
belt and with your right hand also seize his right wrist.

No. 88. Trick 38. Phase 3

When it is necessary to break an opponent's wrist, begin by bending his thumb backward. The thumb is to be bent in the direction that it would go if you were trying to lay it over upon the outer edge of the forearm, and the pressure is applied against the ball of the thumb, just as if it were the nail of the thumb that you wished to make touch first against the outer edge of the forearm. This direction for bending the thumb should be studied carefully. When you have thrown your opponent, as shown in illustration No. 88, press your lower head and neck firmly against his shoulder. At the same time twist your right foot around his right foot in order to complete your secure hold on your victim. Now, all is ready for the application of " submission." With your left hand apply pressure as if to break your victim's thumb, as described above. Fold the fingers of your right hand over your victim's palm and press the ball of your right thumb against the back of his captured hand at a point now to be described. Follow with the ball of your thumb the line between the roots of the two middle fingers. Not quite half-way down the back of the hand your thumb tip will come to a point where the bones appear to join. Severe pressure here with your thumb will cause pain. (Of course practice must be had until this spot can be located instantly.) With the hold secured with your right thumb and fingers, twist your victim's wrist until he surrenders. Study the illustration carefully.

**No. 89. Trick 39. Phase 1**

With your right hand seize your opponent at his left arm, with your thumb thrust inside his sleeve. With your left hand seize his left lapel, then using your left elbow to press forcibly against his right chest just inside the shoulder. This prevents your opponent from closing in with you.

**No. 90.   Trick 39.   Phase 2**

Suddenly release your right-hand hold, if necessary throwing off your opponent's arm as described in Trick 22.   Your right hand now seizes your victim's left lapel.   With your left hand let go altogether.   Now, turn swiftly so that your left side is to your victim. With your right hand drag him over your shoulder.   With your left hand seize him at the back of his right knee.

**No. 91.  Trick 39.  Phase 3**

Your victim thinks he is to be thrown over your shoulder, and naturally he pulls back to resist.   As he does so, throw yourself over backward.   This lands the victim on his back, while you lie on your back across his body.

No. 92.  Trick 40.  Phase 1

Your opponent may seize you at your side, throwing both arms around your waist, as shown in illustration No. 92. Now, throw your right arm over your assailant's right shoulder and with your right hand seize him at his trousers-strap, top of trousers, or at belt in rear. With your left hand seize his right forearm. Wrap your right leg around his left leg as shown in the illustration.

**No. 93.   Trick 40.   Phase 2**

Lowering your body, with your left hand seize your opponent at the inside of his right knee.

No. 94.  Trick 40.  Phase 3

Now release your right leg, which has been wrapped around your opponent's left leg, and step your right leg well outside his left. Throw yourself backward, at the same time lifting his captured right knee.  As you touch the ground your right arm necessarily administers a severe shock to your victim's neck, but it may be necessary to follow up your advantage by employing Trick 41.

**No. 95.  Trick 41.  Phase 1**

When you have thrown your victim by means of the preceding trick, you have fallen with your right knee pressing against the back of his head.  Your right arm is around his neck and your upper right arm presses severely against his upper jaw just under the nose. Wrap your left arm around his left arm so that your hand rests on his back.  Thus your victim is held helpless, and the pressure against his upper jaw forces him to surrender.

No. 96.  Trick 42.  Phase 1

Study the exact positions of the contestants in illustration No. 96, as they face each other for the encounter.

**No. 97. Trick 42. Phase 2**

As you try to seize your adversary's lapel he counters by seizing your wrist, as shown in illustration No. 97.

# Kano Jiu-Jitsu

No. 98. Trick 42. Phase 3

Your opponent now swings, bringing your captured arm over his shoulder as if he intended to throw you by the trick known to American wrestlers as the " flying mare." This " flying mare " is worthless as a *jiu-jitsu* trick. The Japanese employ it only as a ruse. It will be seen, in illustration No. 98, that your opponent has seized your captured hand in such a way that he can bend it over on the wrist to cause pain.

## Trick 42

**Phase 4.** (No illustration.) Your opponent pretends to try to throw you over his shoulder. You drag back and bend back in an effort to throw him. Just as you do so your adversary suddenly slips his head out from under your arm, and, still holding your captured hand, steals back of you. As soon as he is at your rear he applies a crushing flexion that bends your captured hand over upon your wrist. At the same time he extends his right leg, wedging his right foot against the back of your right foot. With your right foot thus wedged, and with his flexing grip on your right hand, he throws you easily, and, if he does so roughly, breaks your right wrist and elbow.

**No. 99.  Trick 43.  Phase 1**

Suppose your opponent actually tries to throw you by the " flying mare"—do not resist by dragging back.  If you do, your opponent will use upon you the foregoing trick.  *This warning is highly important!*  As he attempts to pull you over his shoulder, leap up as if to go over in the way that he wishes you to do.  But press the ball of your left thumb forcibly into the flesh at the top of his left hip bone, and you will cause him such pain that he is weakened, and cannot throw you.

**No. 100. Trick 43. Phase 2**

As your opponent weakens and lets your feet come back to the ground, step your left foot outside and forward of his left foot. At the same instant drag your captured right arm back, and with your left hand seize him under his left knee, thus lifting him and throwing your victim. It may be necessary, now, to employ Trick 44.

# Kano Jiu-Jitsu

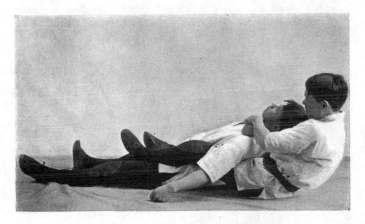

No. 101. Trick 44. Phase 1

As you fall by means of the foregoing trick, wrap your legs crushingly around your victim's waist line. Take hold of his coat lapels with crossed hands and apply strangulation, as shown in illustration No. 101. At the same time, bending your head forward, push the upper portion of your chest against the back of your adversary's head, as shown.

**No. 102.  Trick 45.  Phase 1**

If your assailant seizes your left sleeve with his right hand and throws his left arm around your waist, then throw your right arm around his neck, and with your left hand seize him at his right elbow. In illustration No. 102 the white-belted assailant has placed his left leg back of his opponent's right leg with the intention of throwing the latter backward.

No. 103.  Trick 45.  Phase 2

Your assailant will now take the best hold that seems open to him; he will seize your belt at your left with both of his hands.   Your left hand should now slide down to a grip upon his right wrist.   At the same time, in order to deceive him as to your intentions, wrap your right leg around his left leg, as shown in illustration No. 103.

**No. 104.   Trick 45.   Phase 3**

Now that your assailant is guarding against the grapple that you have taken on his left leg, release your right leg and step it quickly outside of his right leg, at the same time bringing your left leg between his legs, as shown in illustration No. 104.   With your left hand seize the outside of his left knee.

**No. 105. Trick 45. Phase 4**

Sink quickly and forcibly to the right knee. This brings your
victim over, standing on the top of his head. With your right arm
pressing heavily against the back of his head, and your right knee
pushing at the side of your victim's head, throw him over on his
back.

**No. 106. Trick 45. Phase 5**

The fall is made as shown in illustration No. 106. Force your victim's right arm backward over your right knee, as if to break his arm, and continue this pressure until he surrenders.

**No. 107. Trick 46. Phase 1**

Here the assailant (in the white belt) has wrapped both arms around his adversary's waist, and has allowed his opponent (in the black belt) to secure a chancery hold. It is the intention of the man wearing the white belt to throw his opponent backward over his shoulder by means of Trick 38. When attacked in this manner, release your right arm from its chancery hold, and with your right hand seize your opponent at his back strap or belt. Wrap your right leg around his left leg, forcing his foot up from the floor, as shown in illustration No. 107. Bending your knees somewhat, and swaying to the right, throw yourself backward. Fall with your victim under you, and your right arm crushing his neck. In the Second Section many tricks will be explained, by the use of any one of which you will be able to dispose of your antagonist when you have made a throw like this one.

**No. 108. Trick 47. Phase 1**

If your opponent attempts to throw you by the use of Trick 9, release your left arm from its hold around his waist, and throw your left arm around his right arm, as shown in illustration No. 108. This seizure with your left arm will require careful study before you can master it. Your arm is to be held so that it forms like a letter " V," with the fist up, and the base of this " V " is at the back of his upper arm just above the elbow. Now, with your right hand you seize your left wrist. It is not always necessary to employ your other hand to seize the wrist; in this you must be governed by the conditions.

No. 109.   Trick 47.   Phase 2

Like a flash you must fall to your right knee, and extend your left leg, rigid, in front of his left foot.   With your left arm you have a pressure upon his right arm that can be applied forcibly.   Swaying your body a little around to the left, exert this pressure quickly and throw your adversary over your left foot.   This whole trick must be performed with the utmost rapidity.   When your opponent is thus thrown you will find it necessary to employ Trick 48.

No. 110.   Trick 48.   Phase 1

By use of the foregoing trick you threw your antagonist, as shown in illustration No. 110.   Your left arm is still around his right in a " V."   Wrap your left thumb, if possible, in his lapel, and press your left fingers against your victim's " Adam's apple " in order to strangle him.   Wedge your left knee against the back of his right elbow, and apply a twisting pressure with your left arm on his right arm in a way that will break it if he does not promptly surrender. At the time of taking this hold bend over your victim, as shown in the illustration, and push your right hand against his left shoulder in order to prevent his turning.

**No. 111. Trick 49. Phase 1**

If your opponent, with his right hand, seizes your left lapel, and with his left hand your right shoulder, then take the hold shown in illustration No. 111, with your left hand wrapped in his right sleeve and your right hand seizing his *right* lapel. This latter is a bit of strategy, as, from your having seized his right lapel, your opponent thinks it to be your intention to throw him to his right.

**No. 112.   Trick 49.   Phase 2**

Make a quick move to your opponent's left, thrusting your left leg back of his left leg, as shown in illustration No. 112.   At the same time force your head under your adversary's left arm, and with your left hand seize him at the inside of his left thigh.   Now, instantly, shift so as to bring your left leg in front of your opponent's left leg, and your left foot between his two feet.   This is done in order to deceive your adversary, who, when your leg was back of his, had a chance to throw you backward.

**No. 113. Trick 49. Phase 3**

Bend quickly, and shifting to the hold shown opposite, throw your victim over your shoulder. Then employ one of the tricks that you will learn in the first part of the Second Section.

**No. 114. Trick 50. Phase 1**

Here your opponent has seized you with his right hand around your neck, and your left hand has seized him at his right shoulder. If he attempts to seize you with his left hand, strike away that hand by hitting him sharply at the edge of his wrist with the little finger edge of your right hand.

**No. 115. Trick 50. Phase 2**

No appreciable time can elapse between Phase 2 and Phase 3. Both must be performed like lightning. Take off your opponent's right arm by striking his " funny-bone " with your left fist.

**No. 116. Trick 50. Phase 3**

With a sudden turn, throw your left leg back of him and between his two legs, as shown in illustration No. 116. At the same time throw right forearm back of his right leg, and with your left hand seize your own right wrist.

**No. 117.   Trick 50.   Phase 4**

Now, straighten yourself up swiftly, dragging your victim's right leg up with you.   At the same instant press your left elbow strongly against your victim's stomach, and thrust your left foot around outside of his left foot, wedging the latter.   Now, throw yourself backward, carrying your victim over so that he falls under you.   In order to complete the subjugation of your victim, employ Trick 51.

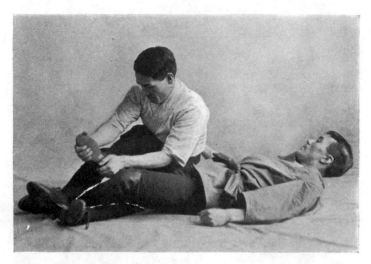

**No. 118. Trick 51. Phase 1**

As soon as your victim is down, wrap your feet around his left foot, as shown in illustration No. 118. Seize your antagonist's right foot just as is shown in the illustration. Bend his knee by pressing your chest against it, and this, aided by twisting the foot, twists his knee as well. The ankle can be broken by this twisting. (This trick is used in wrestling, not against a boxer. But if the victim were to use his idle hand to strike the victor in the neck, the agony caused by having his foot and knee twisted would weaken him so that he would quickly desist from attempting blows.)

**No. 119.  Trick 52.  Phase 1**

With the right hand seize your opponent's right lapel as if you intended to choke him.

**No. 120. Trick 52. Phase 2**

Now, close in with your adversary, and, with your left hand, seize his left coat lapel lower down than you have taken the right lapel. You are now in position to choke your opponent. While taking the hold you have thrown your left leg well past your opponent's, as shown in illustration No. 120.

**No. 121. Trick 52. Phase 3**

Quickly swing sideways and let go of the lapel hold with your left hand, seizing, instead, at your opponent's right side, as shown in illustration No. 121. Throw him over in front of you, the right hand all the while retaining the choking hold with which you began. Subdue your victim by the use of one of the tricks in the first part of the Second Section.

**No. 122.  Trick 53.  Phase 1**

When your antagonist seizes you, as shown in illustration No. 122, with his left hand at the back of your right shoulder, employ your right hand in quickly seizing his right lapel.  Do not allow him to seize you with his right hand.  (If an assailant attempts to seize you at the elbow, strike his hand away with your elbow just as he seizes. Should he attempt to seize your arm higher up, strike the edge of his wrist smartly with the edge of your hand.)

[126]

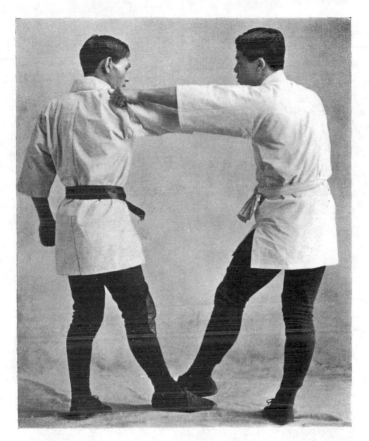

No. 123. Trick 53. Phase 2

Draw back, straightening your right leg and pulling your adversary slightly toward you. This move leads him to think that he has an opportunity, and as he is pulled toward you he slips his left foot outside your right, and prepares to throw you to your right. Quickly shift your right foot outside his left.

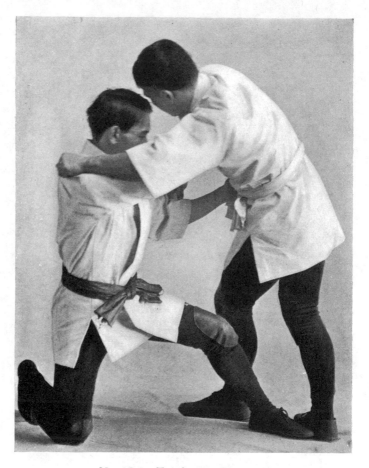

**No. 124.  Trick 53.  Phase 3**

As you close in and seize at your opponent's belt, sink to your right knee and wedge your left knee against the outside of your adversary's left knee.

**No. 125. Trick 53. Phase 4**

This work must be done swiftly and forcefully. With your right hand still at your adversary's right lapel, pull toward you and down, and with your left hand at his right belt, yank strongly up. Throw yourself forward on your right shoulder, and with your left shoulder push your victim's left knee up. Throw him over your left shoulder. Now, follow up your advantage by using Trick 54.

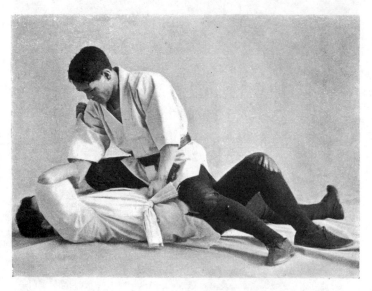

**No. 126. Trick 54. Phase 1**

When the throw has been made by means of the foregoing trick, retain the original hold at your victim's lapel and belt. With your right hand pull the victim's lapel over his throat so that with the second knuckles of your first and second fingers you can press severely against his " Adam's apple." At the same time, with your left hand in the victim's belt, work upward against his stomach with the knuckles at the bases of the phalanges. This motion is difficult of description in words. It is a half-digging, half-churning motion. Roughly knead the victim's stomach and force it upward out of place. This latter trick can be made to cause intense discomfort to the victim. If you were to oppress him only by choking him with your right hand, the victim might escape, but with the stomach attack added he is helpless and must surrender.

No. 127. Trick 55. Phase 1

When your opponent seizes you around the waist, throw your right arm around him and with your left hand seize his right elbow. Now, quickly throw off your opponent's left arm with your right elbow, and throw your right arm around his neck, reaching over and completing your hold by clutching his right lapel with your right hand.

**No. 128.  Trick 55.  Phase 2**

With the back of your right knee kick at the back of your opponent's right knee, forcing him to sit down backward.

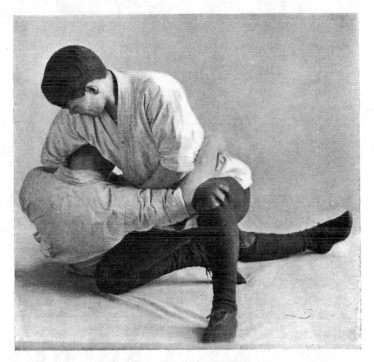

No. 129.  Trick 55.  Phase 3

Your victim will fall as shown in illustration No. 129.  Your right arm is already around his neck.  Now, seize your own right wrist with your left hand, at the same time throwing yourself to a kneeling position at your victim's right.  The victim's neck is just under your shoulder.  Now, tighten up the " V " that you have made with your right arm, and throw your weight upon the back of your victim's neck, at the same time strangling him by the pressure of your forearm at the front of his neck.  This combination of weight and pressure, if carried too far, will break the victim's neck.

**No. 130. Trick 56. Phase 1**

When your assailant seizes your wrist, it is easy to break his hold. Clench your captured fist with the thumb uppermost, and flex the fist up toward your shoulder, keeping the thumb uppermost throughout. In this way you can always break an opponent's hold on your wrist. As you break the hold, seize his wrist instead.

**No. 131.   Trick 56.   Phase 2**

Like a flash your adversary tries to strike you in the face with his free right hand.   Push his captured left fist under his right fist.

**No. 132. Trick 56. Phase 3**

Seize your adversary's crossed wrists with both your hands, swing around, bringing both of his arms over your right shoulder, and throw him.

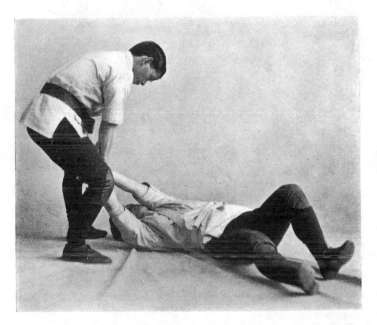

**No. 133. Trick 56. Phase 4**

As the man is thrown, his position and yours will be as shown in illustration No. 133. While the victim's hands are still crossed, seize either one of his thumbs, and now employ Trick 57.

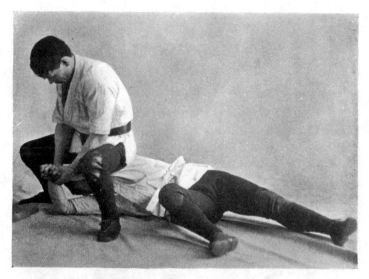

**No. 134. Trick 57. Phase 1**

Here the assailant has seized the right thumb, and has twisted it outward and backward. So far, the hold on both of the victim's hands has been retained. Now, suddenly release the hold on the right thumb, seizing the victim's left wrist with both of your hands. As you do so, suddenly place your left foot at his left arm, and sit down quickly on his left shoulder. Press his left elbow with your left knee and pull his left arm upward. It is possible, in this way, to break the victim's captured arm.

No. 135. Trick 58. Phase 1

Here your assailant has seized you by both wrists.

**No. 136. Trick 58. Phase 2**

If your opponent is very strong, it will be necessary to push strongly down and forward with your captured hands, forcing him to extend his arms straight and rigid, at the same time making him bend backward a little. Now, with your thumbs uppermost, flex your fists and pull your wrists out of his grasp. Then instantly seize his wrists.

**No. 137. Trick 58. Phase 3**

Crossing your adversary's wrists, pull both of his arms over your
shoulder and throw him.

**No. 138. Trick 59. Phase 1**

When your opponent bends forward and wraps both his arms around one of your legs, seize his belt at the back, as shown in illustration No. 138.

No. 139.  Trick 59.  Phase 2

Bring your left foot one step forward, and catch at your adversary's right knee with your left hand.

[143]

**No. 140. Trick 59. Phase 3**

Like a flash throw yourself on the knee that has been seized. At the same time push up on the victim's knee that you have seized, and throw him. Your victim, in a serious contest, lands upon his face, badly damaging it, and as you throw him over upon his back his right elbow is broken.

**No. 141.  Trick 60.  Phase 1**

When your opponent has you in hold at your shoulder, thrust
your arm inside of his and seize him at the back of the neck.

**No. 142. Trick 60. Phase 2**

With your right hand still at the back of your adversary's neck, thrust your left arm between his legs, seizing him at the back of the leg. Swiftly drop to your right knee, push the top of your head against his chest, and extend your left leg between his two legs, wedging your left foot at the back of his left heel. If you do not thus wedge your opponent's left foot he will find a chance to get out of the trap that you have set for him.

No. 143.   Trick 60.   Phase 3

Bend forward, pulling on your victim's collar and on his left leg, as shown in illustration No. 143.   Now throw your man over in front of you on to his back, his feet describing the arc of a circle as he goes over.

# SECTION II

# Kano Jiu-Jitsu

**No. 144. Trick 1. Phase 1**

This is employed when you may find it necessary or advisable to throw yourself down upon your back in order to defeat your assailant. If he advances his left foot forward, roll on to your right side, with your right foot upon the ground and with your left foot in the air at about the height of your adversary's knee. Should your opponent advance with his right foot forward, your right foot should be in the air and your left on the ground. When it is necessary to turn quickly, in order always to keep your feet to your adversary, move with both hands on the ground at your sides. When expecting your opponent to close in, if it happens that your right foot is on the ground and your left foot in the air, then have your left hand on the ground at your side, while your right hand is raised slightly, as shown in illustration No. 144. Thus your hands are always ready to aid you in quickly meeting any attack possible.

**No. 145. Trick 1. Phase 2**

Give your opponent a seeming opportunity to close in upon you. If he does so with his left foot forward, hook your right foot back of his left ankle, and press hard with your left foot against the outside of his left knee. This, when done with force, throws your victim violently over upon the back of his head.

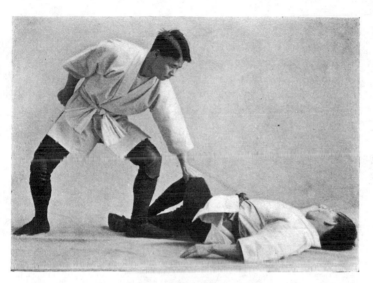

**No. 146.   Trick 2.   Phase 1**

This trick teaches how to overcome an antagonist who employs the preceding trick.   When your opponent is lying in wait for you, with his left foot in the air, advance your own left foot as if intending to dart to the right side of his body.   Instead of doing so, jump over swiftly to his left, hitting down his left knee with your left hand, as shown in illustration No. 146.

## Trick 2.  Phase 2

The push that you give at your opponent's knee renders it impossible for him to employ that leg.  Come instantly down to your knees so that your left knee wedges your adversary's left upper thigh.  At the same time, with your right hand, seize his left wrist.

## Trick 2.  Phase 3

Force your adversary's left fist to the ground as you spring over his body, wedging your left knee under his right elbow.  Throw your left arm tightly around your antagonist's neck.  Now hold your opponent's left hand firmly to the floor, push hard with your left knee against his right elbow, and apply a tight squeeze at the neck. This holds your adversary powerless and forces him to submission.

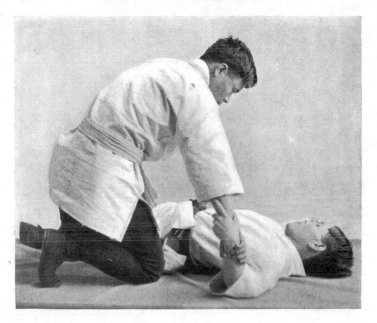

No. 147. Trick 2. Phase 2

No. 148. Trick 2. Phase 3

### Trick 3. Phase 1

While you are lying on your side, if your opponent succeed in closing in at the right side of your body, as shown in illustration No. 149, he will kick at your left knee with his right foot, and then go down on his left knee in position at your right, and will proceed to overcome you.

### Trick 3. Phase 2

As he comes down, push your left knee against his body and catch his right wrist with your left hand. At the same time wrap your right arm around his right calf. Now, with your right arm you are able to twist his right leg, holding it up close to your chest. At the same time you push away his body with your left knee. Thus is your antagonist's move frustrated and he is powerless to win a victory.

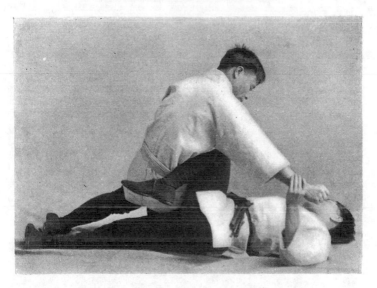

No. 149. Trick 3. Phase 1

No. 150. Trick 3. Phase 2

**No. 151. Trick 4. Phase 1**

Here your opponent has tried to deceive you. He has advanced on his left foot, which causes you to throw your left leg in the air. As he does so, he lands his right foot between your legs, as shown in illustration No. 151. As he does so, with your left hand seize your adversary's right ankle, and with your right hand seize his forefoot. Twist this captured foot severely, and with your left foot push against his right knee. This results in throwing your assailant backward.

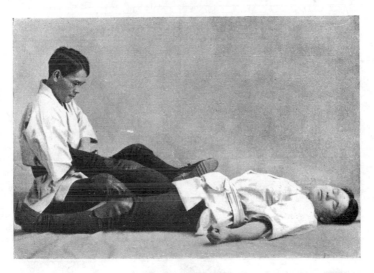

No. 152.   Trick 4.   Phase 2

Follow up your victory by sitting up quickly as your opponent goes over.   Throw your right arm around his left leg just at the bottom of the calf where the fat muscle merges into the tendon. Here the muscle is tender.   Pin his right foot under your right shoulder and twist with the pressure at the bottom of his calf.   Your right knee is under your adversary's right knee, and your foot rests at the bottom of his crotch, or, if need be, squarely against his crotch.   Continue the twisting of your antagonist's right leg, and make the pressure with your right foot as hard as is necessary in order to force your adversary to surrender.

**No. 153. Trick 5. Phase 1**

Here, while you are lying on the ground, your opponent has succeeded in getting past your feet at your right. It is necessary, now, to allow your adversary to take the hold that he wishes.

**No. 154. Trick 5. Phase 2**

Your opponent has elected to begin by seizing your left lapel with his right hand. As he does so, with your right hand seize his right knee, with your left hand seize his right sleeve, and with your left foot push against his chest.

**No. 155.  Trick 5.  Phase 3**

Your opponent will now try to advance on his left foot, getting his head close to yours.  Retaining your hold at his elbow with your left hand, employ your right hand in seizing his left wrist.  Now roll quickly over to your own left.

**No. 156. Trick 5. Phase 4**

The roll over brings you to the position shown in illustration No. 156. Twist your adversary's captured wrist. With your other hand seize your antagonist at the shoulder, resting your elbow at his back. Now push at his shoulder and back, forcing him over on to his other shoulder.

**No. 157. Trick 5. Phase 5**

Wedge your left knee under your opponent's right shoulder, or at his elbow. At the same instant slip your left hand from his shoulder down to his elbow. Now, with your right hand flex your adversary's right hand over upon his wrist, breaking the wrist if the contest be serious enough to make it necessary.

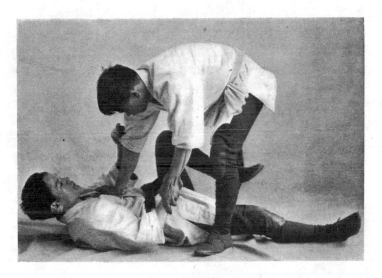

No. 158. Trick 6. Phase 1

While on the ground, allow your antagonist a chance to step over you for a hold, his body just over your knees and his feet outside your legs. As your adversary, with his right hand, seizes one of your lapels, use your left hand to seize his right elbow. Now bend your left leg, thrusting your left foot between your opponent's knees.

### Trick 6.   Phase 2

The first thing needful is to throw off the clutch of your adversary's left hand.   Do this by flexing your captured arm swiftly, with the thumb uppermost, as explained in some of the foregoing tricks, and wrenching your hand free of your opponent's clutch.   With your released right hand seize your antagonist's left lapel, and bring your left foot up into his stomach.

### Trick 6.   Phase 3

Now, extend your left leg forcibly, at the same time pulling your hands to your chest.   This forces your antagonist to stand abruptly on his head.   This, in itself, will constitute a victory, as your adversary will be dazed by the concussion of his head against the ground; but if you wish to make him touch on both shoulders, roll over on him to your right at the instant that he lands on his head, and he will fall on both shoulders.

No. 159. Trick 6. Phase 2

No. 160. Trick 6. Phase 3

### Trick 7.   Phase 1

Here, as you lie on the ground, your opponent has secured an excellent form of hold against you.   With his right hand he has seized your left lapel and is forcing it across your " Adam's apple," choking you.   With his left hand he has seized your right elbow.

### Trick 7.   Phase 2

Twisting your body over to the left, bring your right knee against the outside of your opponent's left buttock.   At the same time relieve yourself from the choking by seizing your adversary's right sleeve with your left hand.   Push your antagonist's left shoulder with your right hand, roll over to your own left, and, by your combined attack, throw your adversary over yourself to your left side.

No. 161. Trick 7. Phase 1

No. 162. Trick 7. Phase 2

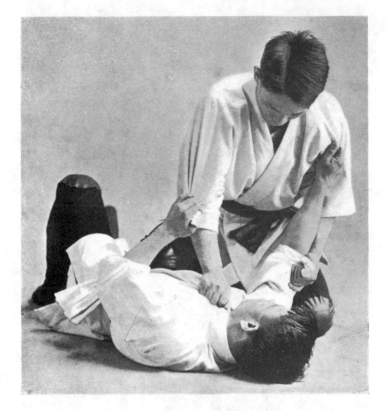

No. 163. Trick 7. Phase 3

As your victim rolls over you and goes down on his shoulders, follow up your advantage by rising and kneeling over him. Your left hand still retains its hold at his right elbow. Bring your left knee up under his right shoulder, wedging it tightly. Pull hard on his right sleeve. As you fall upon him press your right knee into his stomach, and with your right hand seize at his left lapel, forcing it across his throat and choking him.

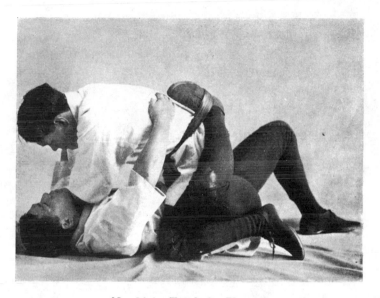

**No. 164. Trick 8. Phase 1**

Here your assailant is endeavouring to choke you. Thrust your
right foot in his belt, as shown, and, by extending your right leg, push
him away. Of course this trick is generally used only when the contestants are wearing the coats and belts of the *jiu-jitsu* costume. It
may, however, be duplicated by pushing one foot in under the lower
edge of a buttoned jacket or vest.

## Trick 9.   Phase 1

Here your opponent over you has taken a crossed-arm hold for a choke, his left hand thus seizing your left lapel, and his right hand your right lapel.

## Trick 9.   Phase 2

Suppose it is your opponent's right forearm that is uppermost while he is administering this choke with his arms crossed before your throat.   Then force your right arm over his left arm and under his right arm at the elbow.   Put your own left hand against your right hand.   (If his left arm were uppermost, it would be necessary to reverse the directions, bringing your own left arm over his right and under his left arm.)

No. 165.  Trick 9.  Phase 1

No. 166.  Trick 9.  Phase 2

### Trick 9.  Phase 3

Here comes a feature which is so important that, if it be forgotten, the trick cannot be performed.  Your assailant still has his hands at the sides of your throat.  Twist your head around to your right, using your jaw-bone to imprison his right hand, and thus hold it fast at the side of your neck.  If possible, wrap your left leg around your assailant's right leg.  Now, make a quick roll to your right, carrying your opponent's body over with you and forcing him to touch on both shoulders.

### Trick 9.  Phase 4

If your assailant succeed in thwarting your attempt to put him on his back, and land on one shoulder only, as shown in illustration No. 168, then press hard against the back of his right elbow, as if to break the elbow.  Your opponent is now forced to take off his left hand.

No. 167. Trick 9. Phase 3

No. 168. Trick 9. Phase 4

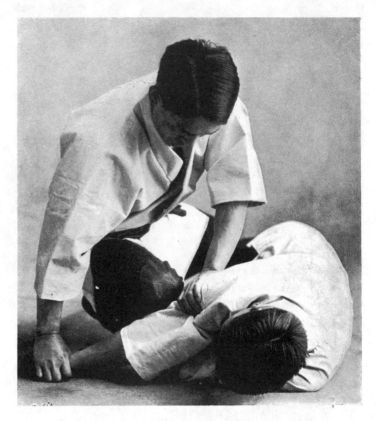

**No. 169. Trick 9. Phase 5**

When your opponent releases his left hand, spring up and over him, seizing his right wrist with your own right hand and his right upper arm with your left hand. At the same time press your right knee against the back of your victim's elbow. If necessary, you can break your victim's arm by this knee pressure.

**No. 170. Trick 10. Phase 1**

Here your opponent has seized your coat lapels and is choking you. With his right hand he has seized your left lapel, and is forcing it across and against your " Adam's apple." With his left hand he has seized your right lapel, lower down than the left lapel, and is pulling it obliquely across to your left.

Trick 10.   Phase 2

Seize your assailant at both wrists, taking such hold that your finger tips dig severely into the inside of each wrist just past the pulse and toward the median line of the wrist. (Practise taking this hold so that it will cause severe pain.)

Trick 10.   Phase 3

Raise one knee, forcing that upper leg against your opponent's back and forcing him to bend forward on you, at the same time aiding this movement by your clutch on his wrists.

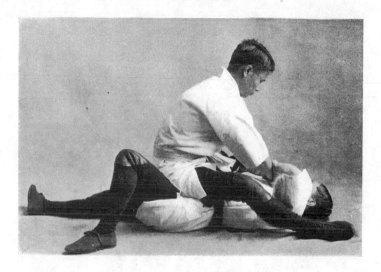

No. 171.  Trick 10.  Phase 2

No. 172.  Trick 10.  Phase 3

**No. 173. Trick 10. Phase 4**

Suddenly take your assaulting knee away, falling back flat and turning quickly and jerkily to the right. At the same time change your right hand swiftly to your adversary's right wrist, and with your left hand secure hold at the back of his right arm just above the elbow. This hold on the right arm is to aid the swift turning movement to the right. With the leverage that you thus obtain you are able to throw your assailant over you and on to his back.

**No. 174.  Trick 10.  Phase 5**

Your adversary falls upon his left shoulder.  Your left hand has hold at his right elbow.  With your own right hand reach across and seize your opponent's right thumb.

**No. 175.  Trick 10.  Phase 6**

The " taking-off " and twisting of a thumb are likely to be puz-
zling to an Occidental mind.  Careful attention must be given to
this phase of *jiu-jitsu*.  Where your opponent's thumb is tightly
wrapped in your cloth, begin by pressing the ball of your thumb
against the *extreme end* of your adversary's thumb nail, at the
same time pressing as if to double the thumb over on itself.  When
this pressure is given at the extreme thumb-nail-end the pain is
sufficient to make your adversary relax his hold with his thumb.
Now, quickly push the ball of your thumb around the inside of your
antagonist's thumb, wrapping the little finger edge of your hand
around the base of his thumb.  The direction of the twist is across
the palm of his hand.  In this phase of the trick push your man's
elbow down and complete the twisting of his thumb by bringing the
palm side of his captured hand up.

[182]

No. 176.   Trick 11.   Phase 1

Here the man on top has secured an excellent fall.   His left hand has taken a strong hold at his victim's right sleeve.   Note the assailant's hold around his victim's neck.   The assailant's right hand grips at the victim's right shoulder.   The assailant's advantage is such that, by tightening the " V " formed by his right arm, and at the same time forcing his head hard against the left side of the victim's face, the assailant is now able to crush his victim's jaw and to cause agonising pain.

### Trick 11.   Phase 2

Before your opponent can secure the full advantage of the hold shown in the preceding phase—that is, before he has time to complete his advantage by forcing his head against the left side of your face—swiftly throw your feet up over him as high as you can, just as is shown in illustration No. 177.

### Trick 11.   Phase 3

Just as your opponent is ready to resist the move that he thinks you contemplate by throwing your feet up in the air, let your feet quickly return to the floor and your body " collapse " as much as it will.   At the same time force your free left arm in front of your throat and force him over across your body.

No. 177. Trick 11. Phase 2

No. 178. Trick 11. Phase 3

### Trick 11.  Phase 4

It is easy, now, to throw yourself upon your adversary in the manner shown in illustration No. 179.  Your right knee presses severely against his right shoulder.  With your left hand seize his left collar, applying the pressure of your arm across his " Adam's apple."  Your right hand merely helps to hold his body down.

### Trick 12.  Phase 1

If your adversary get you down, as in the last trick, here is another way of disposing of him: With your free left hand push the right side of his neck.

No. 179.  Trick 11.  Phase 4

No. 180.  Trick 12.  Phase 1

Trick 12.   Phase 2

Bring up your left leg against your adversary's neck.   Push him down as shown in illustration No. 181.

Trick 12.   Phase 3

With your left hand seize the left edge of your opponent's coat a little way below the lapel, and with your right hand seize his left wrist.   Now, using your left arm as a fulcrum, bend your antagonist's captured left arm backward so that it is possible to break it.   At the same time squeeze your victim's neck with your legs.

No. 181. Trick 12. Phase 2

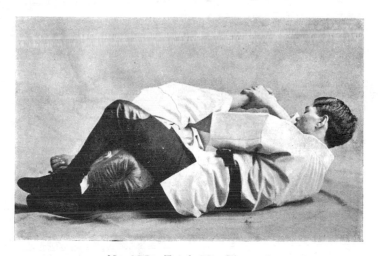

No. 182. Trick 12. Phase 3

### Trick 13. Phase 1

This illustrates another way in which two antagonists may fall. The man on top has his right arm around his opponent's neck, gripping at the right shoulder, and his right knee presses the antagonist's right arm to the floor.

### Trick 13. Phase 2

If you happen to be the under man, push up your assailant's right knee with your right hand. At the same time force your right knee up so that you can press it against his right kidney. Force your left arm against your opponent's " Adam's apple," gripping the cloth at his left shoulder.

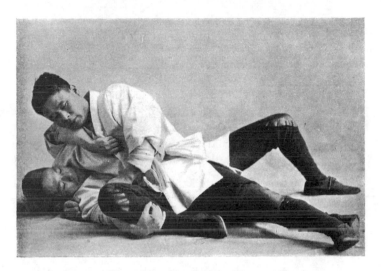

No. 183.   Trick 13.   Phase 1

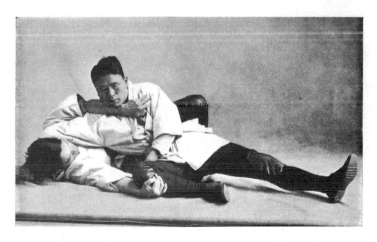

No. 184.   Trick 13.   Phase 2

### Trick 13.  Phase 3

Now it is easy to force your assailant to the position shown in illustration No. 185.  Pull your left arm toward you, pressing roughly against your opponent's " Adam's apple."  With your right hand seize his right lapel.  If your antagonist try to face you, release the pressure with your left arm and, instead, force his right lapel down on his " Adam's apple " with a choking pressure.

### Trick 14.  Phase 1

Here is still another way of getting out of the predicament that is shown in Trick 11, Phase 1.  Force one of your feet through the belt of your assailant.  If your assailant be in street costume, you can force your foot through his back-strap, or in at the top of his trousers.

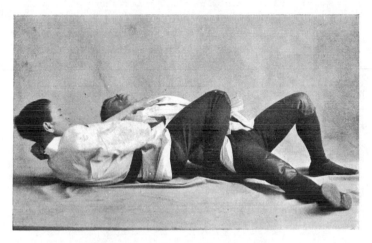

No. 185. Trick 13. Phase 8

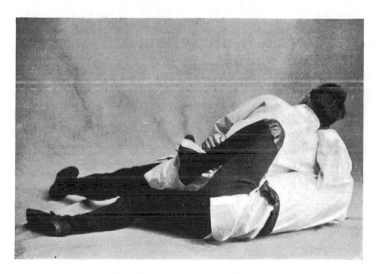

No. 186. Trick 14. Phase 1

### Trick 14. Phase 2

Push, forcing your antagonist down away from you. Now, catch his right thumb and twist it over across the back of his hand. This forces the fingers of the captured hand to follow the thumb. Apply the pressure until you are able to press against the second knuckle of your adversary's little finger, still twisting. In this feat you begin the hold upon the captured hand with your own left hand, and finish when the thumb of your right hand is pressing the second knuckle of the little finger of your opponent's right hand in the manner just described.

### Trick 14. Phase 3

Now, still twisting, get up over your antagonist. Still retaining the hold on your adversary's captured right hand, wedge your right knee just under his right elbow. Press your left thumb in the depression under the lobe of his right ear.

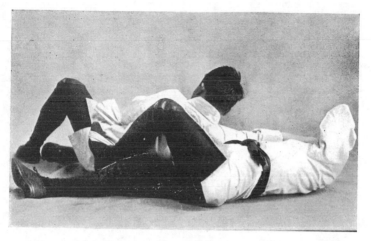

No. 187.  Trick 14.  Phase 2

No. 188.  Trick 14.  Phase 3

### Trick 15.   Phase 1

Here your opponent has thrown you, and resorts to choking you. He has seized one lapel, and intends to seize the other.   Before he can do this, thrust one of your hands between his two hands, and seize the lapel which he intended to take next.   Hold on to your own lapel, and depress your chin strongly.   He cannot choke you now.

### Trick 15.   Phase 2

Use your free left hand to seize your antagonist's left wrist; he will now seize your left wrist with his right hand.

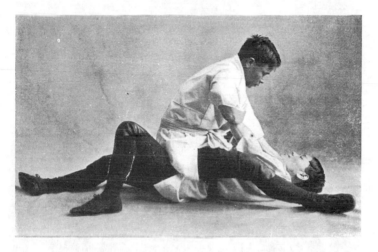

No. 189. Trick 15. Phase 1

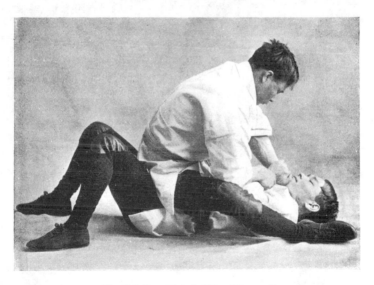

No. 190. Trick 15. Phase 2

**No. 191. Trick 15. Phase 3**

Now press your right knee firmly against your adversary's buttocks, and roll to your left, throwing him over you, as shown in illustration No. 191. Continue this pressure with your right knee so that your antagonist cannot sit up again. At the same time push against his left elbow with your right hand, and with your left jaw hold his captured hand wedged. Your enemy cannot move.

**No. 192. Trick 16. Phase 1**

Here your opponent is shown on top. With his right hand he has hold of your left lapel. With his left hand he has hold of the right edge of your coat just below the lapel. It is his intention to choke you by pressing your left lapel across your " Adam's apple," at the same time pulling your right coat edge obliquely to the left.

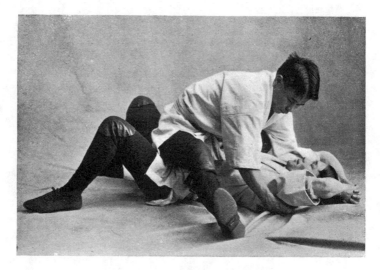

**No. 193. Trick 16. Phase 2**

Thrust your clasped hands between your opponent's two arms. Bring your clasped hands swiftly over back of your head, spreading your elbows as you do so. This breaks your enemy's hold at your throat. Now use Trick 17.

# Kano Jiu-Jitsu

**No. 194. Trick 17. Phase 1**

Quickly bring your knees up and seize your antagonist at lapel
and belt, as shown in illustration No. 194. Push against your man's
stomach, and at the same time raise yourself on your shoulders.
Thus you are able to force your adversary over backward.

**No. 195. Trick 17. Phase 2**

In order to protect himself your opponent must give up the hold that he had.  Seize his legs, as shown in illustration No. 195.  Push his left knee outward and over as far as you can.  While doing this you are holding your adversary's body braced on your knees.  Having spread your adversary's legs, lower your own knees like a flash and pull from under him in order to rise.  In doing this you should throw your man backward in such fashion that both his shoulders touch the floor.

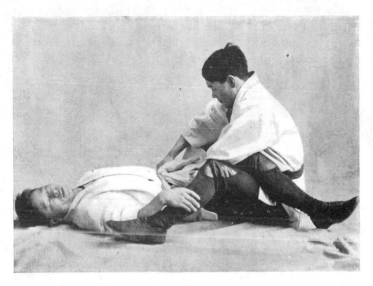

**No. 196.   Trick 17.   Phase 3**

If both his shoulders do not touch as he falls, throw your left arm around under your adversary's right knee, and force his right leg up. This will oblige him to touch on both shoulders.

### Trick 18.   Phase 1

Here the assailant, if he be clever enough, has a good chance to defeat the under man.   If you are downed by such an assault, use your free hand—in this case the right—to seize your assailant at lapel or shoulder and hold him as much as possible away from you.

### Trick 18.   Phase 2

Quickly roll to the left, hooking the back of your left hand back of your adversary's right knee.   With your own right hand push against his knee, as shown in illustration No. 198.   There is an important trick to be caught in connection with this right-hand hold. The point of the thumb should press against a nerve that can be found at the inside of the back of the leg just below the knee joint. This nerve can be found after a little practice on one's own leg. When pressed sharply this nerve responds with a shoot of pain.

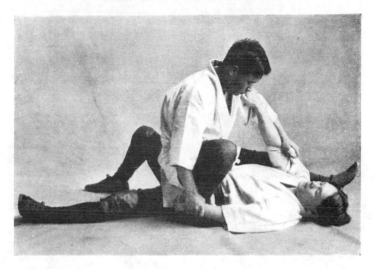

No. 197. Trick 18. Phase 1

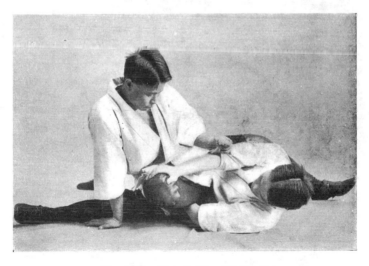

No. 198. Trick 18. Phase 2

**No. 199.  Trick 18.  Phase 3**

Now, throw your right leg over your assailant, as shown in illustration No. 199.   Your leg holds his arm down, and your foot rests upon his chest.   At the same time you have your adversary's right foot under your left arm in such a fashion that by holding his foot pinioned and forcing up your forearm you are able to twist his right foot.

**No. 200. Trick 19. Phase 1**

Here the assailant has secured an excellent hold. He has thrown his adversary, and has fallen so that with his knees he has pinioned the latter's arms. The assailant's right hand has seized the antagonist's left lapel. The assailant's left hand is wrapped in the cloth of the prostrate man's collar, while the assailant's thumb is pressed against the prostrate man's " Adam's apple."

**No. 201. Trick 19. Phase 2**

Relieve the strangulation by depressing your chin strongly against the assailant's hand. Seize his sleeves, as shown in illustration No. 201, and pull his arms quickly and forcibly away from the sides of his body. This is intended only to deceive your antagonist, for he, not knowing what your intentions are, will throw a great deal of strength into his arms in order to resist. Now, quickly bring your knees up, as shown in illustration No. 201, striking your opponent in the back and pitching him forward upon you.

**No. 202.  Trick 19.  Phase 3**

In the first phase your antagonist had been pulled so far over you that it needs only a slight movement to pitch him forward on his head.   This impetus you supply by the start to throw a somersault with your own body.

**No. 203. Trick 19. Phase 4**

As your antagonist goes over he is bound to touch on both shoulders. Now, yank him toward you, holding his knees against you with your arms.

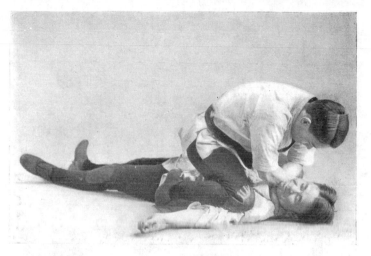

No. 204. Trick 20. Phase 1

In some of the preceding tricks the assailant has been defeated because the best strangle-hold that he knew did not apply to the case. A form of choking is shown here that is excellent. With your right hand seize at your antagonist's collar as far around as you can get it. As soon as you get this hold with your hand wedge your forearm under his chin, as shown in illustration No. 204. Slip your left arm under your own right arm and seize your opponent's left collar. Here the right arm is employed only to keep the adversary's chin up, while the choking is accomplished by pressure with your left arm. As you secure this hold throw your arms and your own body down close to your opponent, and it is important that your elbows all but touch your knees. With your victim's arms pinned, and your hold so taken, your victim has little chance of escape. Should he attempt to roll with you, go with him, all the time keeping up the strangling. His efforts will exhaust him, and the strangling will render him unconscious.

[211]

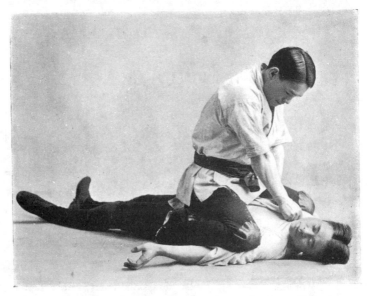

No. 205. Trick 21. Phase 1

Here is a useful strangle-hold. With your right hand grip your victim's left lapel, and with your left hand seize the right edge of his coat below the lapel. Pull the right edge of the victim's coat slantingly across his chest, at the same time digging the second knuckles of the first two fingers of the right hand in at the right side of his "Adam's apple."

Phase 2. (No illustration.) Anticipate your victim's intention to roll to either side by rolling over sideways before he has a chance to make you do it. If you are administering the choking pressure with your right hand, then roll to your right; if with your left hand, then roll to your left. As you go over upon your side throw your uppermost leg around your victim. As you get over on your side, having retained your choking hold, administer the choking by holding your victim at arm's length.

# Kano Jiu-Jitsu

No. 206. Trick 22. Phase 1

When you throw your victim in this position, be careful to throw your own body as well past his head as possible, in order that he may have no chance to make you turn a somersault with him. This precaution is vital to the success of the trick.

Phase 2. (No illustration.) The directions can be understood by studying the photograph of the preceding phase. Your opponent is sure to release his right arm around your neck. Should he attempt to get a hold under your knee with the intention of rolling you over, force his right arm down over your right knee and bend it backward to break it.

Phase 3. (No illustration.) Study the illustration of Phase 1. What is more likely is that your victim will try to push his right arm against the right side of your neck in the effort to push you away from him. Should he attempt this latter move, allow him to get his arm between his head and yours, but as he does so use your left hand to push against his right elbow, thus forcing his right forearm severely against his upper lip and nose. Now, pressing your right shoulder against your victim's right forearm, and taking tight hold of your own right wrist with your left hand, strangle and at the same time complete the crushing pressure of his right forearm against his upper lip and nose.

### Trick 23.  Phase I

Here your victim, upon being thrown, has succeeded in getting his right hand free and under your body.  It is his intention to force you to roll over with him.  Bend quickly over him, throwing the weight of the inside of your shoulder against his nose and upper lip. With your left hand seize your own right wrist, and now give a crushing hug, bearing all the weight you can against your opponent's nose and upper lip.

### Trick 24.  Phase I

Illustration No. 208 all but explains this method of choking.  But when you seize a victim in this way it is all-important to clasp your hands in the right way.  Place your left thumb between your right palm and thumb.  Wrap your left fingers around the back of your right hand, and wrap your right fingers around your left thumb. This leaves no opening exposed for your adversary to wrench your hands away.  In administering the choke draw your clasped hands toward yourself, at the same time leaning well forward and pressing your chest against the point of your victim's head.

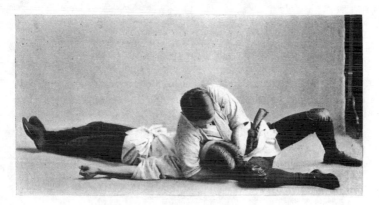

No. 207. Trick 23. Phase 1

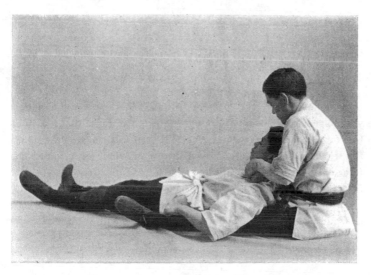

No. 208. Trick 24. Phase 1

### Trick 25.  Phase 1

If you attempt the choke depicted in illustration No. 209, your adversary, having his hands free, will be able to secure a hold on your legs and roll over with you, thus defeating your object.  Quickly spread your legs alongside his body, digging your knees into the soft place just above either hip-bone.  Then lean back and severely complete the pressure at your victim's throat and over his hip-bones.

### Trick 26.  Phase 1

Sometimes, when you attempt to administer the " submission," your opponent will be quick enough to turn his arm so that it cannot be bent backward over your knee.  To meet this emergency employ the trick shown in illustration No. 210.  In falling upon your man force one knee under his captured arm.  Twist the wrist so that he is forced to place his arm with its back against your knee.  At the same time rest your other knee over your adversary's captured fist, and press against it with your knee as well as with your hand.

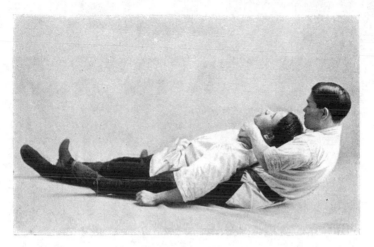

No. 209.  Trick 25.  Phase 1

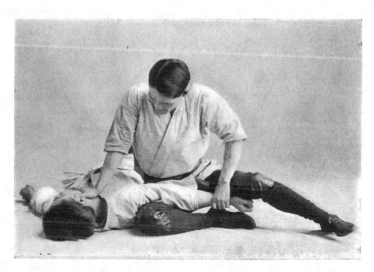

No. 210.  Trick 26.  Phase 1

# Kano Jiu-Jitsu

## Trick 27.   Phase 2

Phase 1.   (No illustration.)   Your opponent has been thrown, and you are sitting astride of him.

Phase 2.   Your adversary reaches up for one of your lapels, and you must seize his thumb or wrist.   Twist either the thumb or wrist and fall over backward at your victim's side.   At the same time wrap your legs around the arm of his captured hand, as shown in illustration No. 211, and bend his arm backward as if to break it over one of your legs.

## Trick 28.   Phase 2

Phase 1.   Same as Phase 1 of the preceding trick.

Phase 2.   Your adversary attempts to take a hold around your body for the purpose of rolling with you and throwing you over sideways. With your right hand, for instance, seize your opponent's left thumb or wrist and twist.   While doing so, force his right arm backward over your right leg, as if to break the arm.   With your left hand apply any one of the chokings already described.

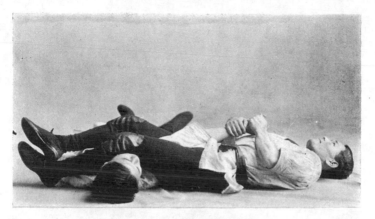

No. 211. Trick 27. Phase 2

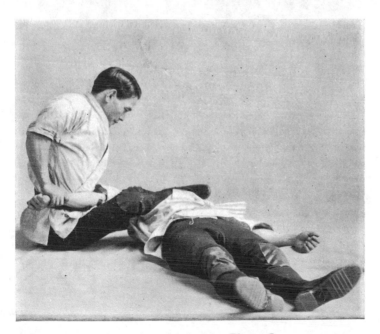

No. 212. Trick 28. Phase 2

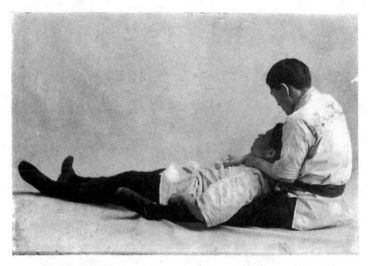

No. 213.  Trick 29.  Phase 2

Phase 1.  (No illustration.)  If you seize your adversary from the
rear to throw him, hook your right arm around his throat.  With your
left hand grip his left elbow.  At the same time butt your opponent in
the small of his back with one of your knees.  Sit down quickly and
drag him backward into your lap.

Phase 2.  Hook your left arm around your opponent's throat, as
shown in illustration No. 213.  The tips of the first two fingers of
your left hand should dig into your adversary's right jugular.  With
your right hand seize one of his lapels in front of your left hand.
Thus your right hand is ready to repel any attack that your adversary may attempt upon your left hand.

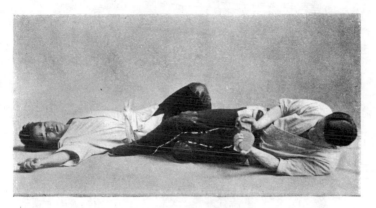

No. 214.   Trick 30.   Phase 2

Phase 1.   (No illustration.)   As you throw your opponent, and bend over him to get a hold, he reaches up with his left hand and seizes the cloth at your right elbow.   With his right hand he seizes your right lapel.   At the instant of taking these holds he thrusts his right foot against your abdomen.   Now he is in position to roll over to his own left, throwing you.

Phase 2.   Seize your adversary's foot and quickly advance your left foot toward your opponent's shoulder.   Now, throw yourself backward and wrap your right leg securely over his captured leg.   With your hands take the holds upon his captured foot that are shown in illustration No. 214.   Twist the foot until your antagonist surrenders.

Phase 3.   (No illustration.)   Instead of throwing yourself backward, as in the preceding phase, simply sit down with your right arm around your adversary's captured leg, so that your right forearm presses against the lower portion of his calf.   Thus your right arm forms a " V," your right fist being in front of your abdomen.   It is the bony, thumb side of your forearm that presses against his lower calf. With your left hand seize your own right wrist, and with this purchase increase the vise-like pressure against his lower calf.   Now, throw yourself over prostrate on your back, and you are able to increase the pressure still more.   This oppression against the tender muscular tissue causes great pain and forces your opponent to submit.

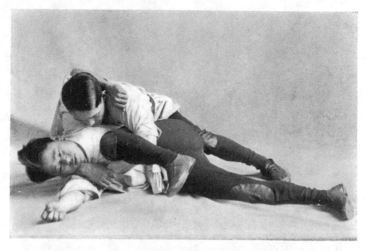

**No. 215. Trick 31. Phase 2**

Phase 1. (No illustration.) Your opponent has endeavoured to throw you by the " flying mare " trick. (See Trick 12, Section I.) As he attempts to throw you over his right shoulder, throw your weight off your feet as in Trick 12, and remember that it is vital not to resist your assailant. But, as your antagonist gets you off your feet, jab your left thumb against the top of his left hip-bone forcibly enough to cause pain. As he weakens and you return to your feet, land with your left foot well in advance of his left foot and your right foot behind his left foot.

Phase 2. Instantly throw your left arm around the back of your opponent's left knee, step quickly back, in order to carry your opponent off his balance, and throw yourself over backward. Thus you carry your opponent down with his left knee pressing forcibly against his left shoulder. Now, with your right hand, seize your own left wrist and complete the pressure on his left knee. At the same time your right forearm may be made to exert a strangling pressure against your opponent's right jugular.

No. 216.  Trick 32.  Phase 1

Here the contestants have taken an ordinary wrestling hold.  The assailant (in the black belt) has pushed against his intended victim as if to place one foot in the victim's abdomen and to throw himself over backward.  This the man in the white belt has countered by advancing a knee to kick his opponent's foremost knee.

**No. 217. Trick 32. Phase 2**

When you are the assailant in such a feat sink quickly to your left knee, and wedge your right knee against your adversary's right knee.

No. 218.  Trick 32.  Phase 3

Like a flash rise, partially, advance your left foot, raise it and plant it against your opponent's right side.  Do not seek to rise to a standing position while doing this.  It must be done so quickly that you are going backward by the time that your foot has landed.

[225]

No. 219.   Trick 32.   Phase 4

It makes no difference whether your hands have seized at your opponent's sleeves or at his lapels.   The result will be the same. Bring your opponent to the position shown in illustration No. 219.

No. 220. Trick 32. Phase 5

Pulling on your victim's left sleeve or lapel, press your left foot hard against his right side, and throw him over back of you over your right shoulder. Should your opponent fail to land on both shoulders employ any one of the tricks described so far in the Second Section that is best suited to the purpose.

**No. 221. Trick 33. Phase 1**

Here you and your opponent have broken hold at one side, and he has placed his left leg outside of your left leg with the intention of throwing you over to your left. Defeat his intention by stooping quickly. At the same time thrust your left arm under his crotch, seizing the cloth at the back of his crotch. Your right arm was at your opponent's left shoulder, but at the instant of taking the crotch-hold release your right hand and push your right forearm against your antagonist's throat, forcing him to a fall over backward.

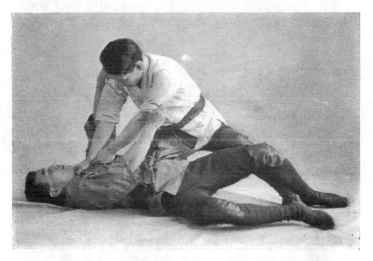

No. 222. Trick 33. Phase 2

Just as your opponent is in the act of falling release your left hand from his crotch and seize his right coat edge. Go over with your victim, landing your right knee hard in his left side. With your right hand take hold very high up on his right collar and pull over hard across his " Adam's apple " in order to strangle him.

**No. 223. Trick 34. Phase 1**

When your opponent attacks you from behind, throwing his arms under your arms and around your waist, throw your right arm around his neck, as shown in illustration No. 223.

**No. 224. Trick 34. Phase 2**

Now, throw your right arm along the length of your opponent's right jaw-bone. With your left hand seize your right wrist, and press his jaw-bone as closely to you as you can. This pressure can be so applied as to give your victim excruciating torment. At the instant of starting this pressure bend your knees, as shown in illustration No. 224.

No. 225. Trick 34. Phase 3

Throw yourself down, squeezing your victim's jaw between your right arm and the portion of your body that is under your right shoulder. The pain can be made so agonizing that the strongest man will have to submit. When you have your antagonist in this predicament, a little twist outward will break his neck.

No. 226. Trick 35. Phase 1

Here your opponent has seized you with his left hand on your belt at the right side. His right hand may have taken hold at any point on your left arm. Throw off your adversary's right hand, as described in tricks in the First Section, and seize either his right wrist or his right thumb. Your right arm takes a hold on your opponent anywhere back of his left shoulder.

**No. 227.  Trick 35.  Phase 2**

Now, swing to one side, as shown in illustration No. 227.   With
your left hand seize your antagonist's left elbow, hooking your right
arm over his left arm, and seizing your own left wrist.   At the same
time kick backward with the back of your right leg against his left
knee.   Throw your adversary forward over your right leg.   When
you have thrown your man, bring about submission by the employment of any of the tricks in the first part of this Section that applies
to the case.

No. 228. Trick 36. Phase 1

Here the assailant has taken a hold that is known in American wrestling as the " Nelson." The assailant has thrust his arms under his antagonist's arms, and has clasped his hands at the back of the other's neck.

**No. 229. Trick 36. Phase 2**

When you are caught in this hold, seize your own left wrist as swiftly as possible. Bring your elbows forcibly down against your sides and bend well forward, thrusting your buttocks well back.

No. 230. Trick 36. Phase 3

Kick with either foot. Here the man assailed is shown kicking with his left foot, which he places back of his antagonist's left foot. The kick is made sharply at the ankle, with a wide, sweeping movement forward. Seize your opponent's left leg in the way shown. Quick as a flash slide your left hand down upon his forefoot. At the same time seize his ankle with your right hand. Yank the foot clear of the floor; twist the foot violently and throw yourself backward. This throws your opponent under you to the floor.

[237]

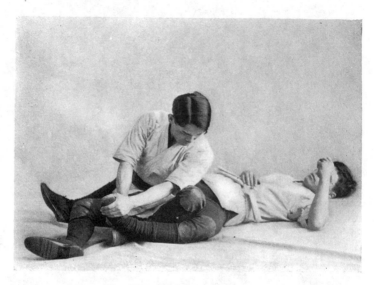

**No. 231. Trick 36. Phase 4**

You will fall upon your antagonist as shown in illustration No. 231. Your weight is upon his right knee, forcing it against his left. Thus the left knee is held wedged in place while you twist your adversary's left foot until he submits.

No. 232.   Trick 36.   Phase 5

In case your opponent attempts to use his right foot for his own defence, slide across his legs in the manner shown above.  Sit on his upper left leg, with your knees wedging his lower left leg in place.  Twist his left foot until submission is secured.

**No. 233. Trick 37. Phase 1**

Make a close study of the assailant's hold as shown in the photograph illustrating Phase 1 of the preceding Trick, and compare it with the " Nelson " hold shown in illustration No. 233. In this latter case the assailant has taken his hold so that his elbows are well forward. When the attack is made in this way, throw your arms around your antagonist's arms above his elbows, then seizing one of your own wrists and bringing your hands quickly and strongly against your own abdomen. But unless you are able to get your arms around your opponent's above his elbows, it is not safe to use this present trick.

**No. 234. Trick 37. Phase 2**

Take one step forward, on either foot as you prefer. Now, throw a somersault with your opponent. If he be squarely on your back, throw yourself straight forward. If your antagonist be a little at your right, throw the somersault to your own left—not squarely to the left, but to the left of a straight forward direction. Should your assailant be behind you, but somewhat at your left, make your somersault to the right of forward. Continued practice in the earlier tricks of Section I. will enable you to throw this somersault with skill.

### Trick 37.   Phase 3

You will fall with your opponent under you, as shown in illustration No. 235.   His hold is broken.   If necessary, in order to hold him, wrap one of your legs around one of his.   Keep your adversary in this position.

### Trick 37.   Phase 4

Seize either of your adversary's hands.   In illustration No. 236 it is the left hand that has been seized.   Take his hand with both of yours, your thumbs pressing against the joint at the back of his wrist.   Swiftly slide your thumbs down to the middle of the back of his hand, and flex the hand over upon his wrist, causing pain. Quickly change to this hold.   Cross your own wrists, and with one of your hands seize his first two fingers, and with your other hand take his other two fingers.   Now, while pulling his two pairs of fingers apart, twist your victim's wrist around severely.   This compels submission.

No. 235.  Trick 37.  Phase 3

No. 236.  Trick 37.  Phase 4

[243]

**No. 237. Trick 38. Phase 1**

Here your assailant has taken a hold from the rear around your neck. Force down your chin as hard as you can upon one of his arms. Do not omit this chin pressure! It is essential to the success of the defence.

**No. 238. Trick 38. Phase 2**

With your right hand seize the cloth at your adversary's right elbow. Throw your left hand back of you, gripping the cloth at the small of his back. Take one step forward on the right foot. Note the relative positions of the feet.

No. 239.  Trick 38.  Phase 3

Bend quickly forward, dragging your opponent off his feet.  Finding himself going, he is bound to release one of his hands for the purpose of saving himself.  As shown in illustration No. 239, it is the left hand that he has released from around your neck.  At this instant seize your opponent's right wrist with your left hand, and hold it against your chest.  In bending forward for the throw be sure that your antagonist's middle is resting upon your buttocks.

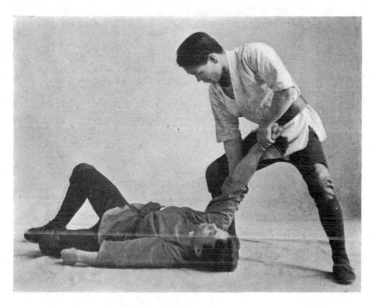

**No. 240. Trick 38. Phase 4**

Do not release any part of your hold, and your victim is thrown exactly as is shown in illustration No. 240.

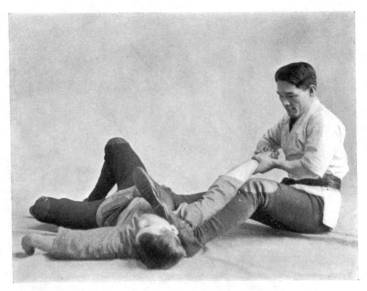

**No. 241. Trick 38. Phase 5**

As your victim attempts to escape from his plight, quickly and strongly stretch his captured arm, at the same time sitting down and pressing your feet against his head and chest. Bend his captured arm backward over one of your knees until your victim submits.

**No. 242. Trick 39. Phase 1**

Here your opponent has seized you from behind, pinning your arms. As shown in the illustration, the hold is taken around your upper arms. In this case step forward on your right foot and throw your right arm obliquely forward and up in the familiar attitude of the American stump orator.

**No. 243. Trick 39. Phase 2**

But if your assailant has pinned your arms at the elbows, then step back, instead, thrusting your left leg between his two legs. With your right hand seize the cloth at your opponent's right shoulder. Wrap your left arm around your adversary's left knee from the outside.

**No. 244. Trick 39. Phase 3**

When you get the hold described in the foregoing, bend well forward, throwing your adversary over your right shoulder. In making the throw go to your right knee.

### Trick 39.   Phase 4

Your victim falls as shown in illustration No. 245.   Retain your original hold, and have your right knee under his right shoulder.

### Trick 39.   Phase 5

Study carefully the position shown in illustration No. 246.   Quickly put down your victim's right hand, and sit on it with your left haunch.   Force your right foot under his right arm in order to wedge his captured wrist.   At the same time hook your right hand under your adversary's right arm just above the elbow.   With your left hand seize your own right wrist and drag your hands up toward your chest.   It is possible, with this combined pressure, to break your opponent's arm.   In order to prevent his turning upon you, press your left foot against his head, as shown.

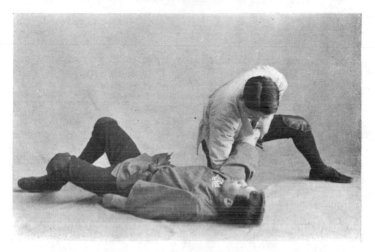

No. 245. Trick 89. Phase 4

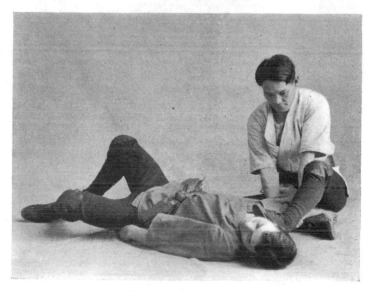

No. 246. Trick 39. Phase 5

**No. 247. Trick 40. Phase 1**

Here your assailant has seized you around your body from the rear, but without pinning your arms.

No. 248. Trick 40. Phase 2

Seizing your adversary's clasped hands with your left hand, grab the cloth at his right elbow with your right hand. Make a quick turn around to your left.

**No. 249.  Trick 40.  Phase 3**

As you swing to your left you force your antagonist off his balance enough to make him step forward on his left foot.   With your own left foot kick the ankle and outside of his left foot.   This is a swinging kick, intended to force your opponent's left foot over to the right.

**No. 250.  Trick 40.  Phase 4**

As your adversary's left foot is kicked over to the right he is bound
to bend his left knee.  With your left hand, as shown in illustration
No. 250, force his left knee outward to the left.  At the same time
push against his upper left leg with your left knee.  Now, as your
opponent goes off his balance, fall to your left, forcing him over with
you.

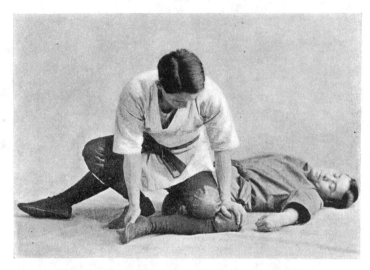

**No. 251. Trick 40. Phase 5**

As your victim falls, hold his left knee with your left hand and left knee, and with your right hand hold his left heel.

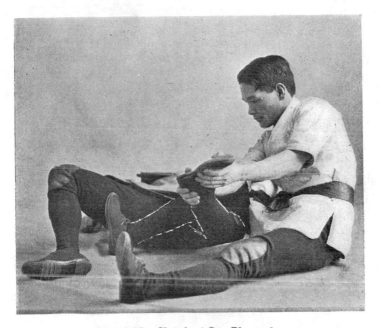

**No. 252. Trick 40. Phase 6**

As your victim attempts to squirm out of his predicament throw
yourself across to the other side of his body, bracing your right foot
against his right upper leg.   With your right hand still at your victim's left heel, with your left hand seize his left forefoot.   Now pull
your victim's captured foot up strongly toward your chest, thus compelling submission.

# Kano Jiu-Jitsu

**No. 253. Trick 41. Phase 1**

Here your opponent has seized you around the body from the
rear, and has wrapped his right leg around your left leg.  It is his
intention to throw you over to your right.  With your right hand
seize the cloth under his right elbow.  With your left hand seize his
right wrist.

**No. 254. Trick 41. Phase 2**

Quickly thrust your left leg back of your assailant's right leg.

**No. 255. Trick 41. Phase 3**

Keeping your adversary's weight on your left leg, bend obliquely forward to the right, and throw your opponent around your own body.

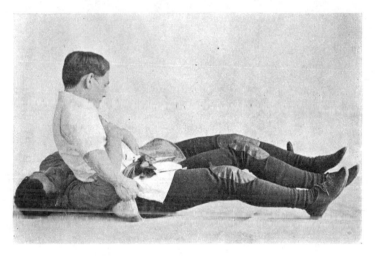

**No. 256. Trick 41. Phase 4**

Your opponent will be thrown to the position shown in illustration No. 256.

**No. 257. Trick 41. Phase 5**

Here is where you deceive your opponent.  In his plight, as shown in the last phase, he imagines that you are going to twist his right hand.  Accordingly he has closed his right hand tightly.  Quickly shift to the position shown in illustration No. 257, and with your right hand seize his left thumb.  With your left hand seize your opponent's left hand so that your fingers are in his palm, while your thumb presses at the back of his hand.  Wedge your left foot against his right shoulder.  Now twist your victim's captured hand over to compel submission.

No. 258. Trick 42. Phase 1

Here your assailant has seized you, at first, from in front. His right hand is on your shoulder, and his left hand has seized the end of your right sleeve with the thumb inside. Now, quickly wheel, presenting your back to him and bringing his right arm over your right shoulder. This is easily done. Your adversary's hold with his left hand is thereby broken, and he takes a new hold with that hand somewhere at your left side.

[265]

No. 259.  Trick 42.  Phase 2

Seize your opponent's sleeves at the elbows, and quickly turn so as to bring your left leg back of his right leg.

**No. 260. Trick 42. Phase 3**

Straighten up and lean over backward. Then throw yourself backward, falling with your opponent under you.

### Trick 42.   Phase 4

The illustration shows the relative positions in which yourself and your opponent will fall.

### Trick 42.   Phase 5

Seize your opponent's right hand under the finger-tips with your own right hand, taking his hand off.

No. 261. Trick 42. Phase 4

No. 262. Trick 42. Phase 5

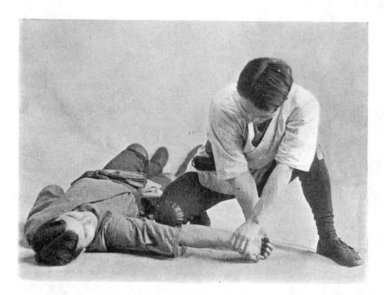

**No. 263. Trick 42. Phase 6**

(By an error the victor's grip on the victim's right fingers is shown to be changed. The grip, as shown in the preceding illustration, should not be changed.) Throw yourself over to the position shown, and seize your victim's wrist with your right hand. Now, twist your opponent's wrist until he submits.

**No. 264. Trick 43. Phase 1**

The position is taken as shown in illustration No. 264, the assailant having taken hold with both arms around his opponent's body. The antagonists do not hug each other closely. When attacked in this fashion, secure a hold on your adversary's right arm, and advance your right foot between his feet.

**No. 265. Trick 43. Phase 2**

While your opponent's arms are around you, throw both of your arms over his at the elbows, seizing one of your own wrists with your other hand, as shown in illustration No. 265. Squeeze your adversary's arms inward together so that he cannot escape; in doing so, pull your own arms up to you as close as possible. Bring up your left knee forcefully against your adversary's stomach.

**No. 266. Trick 43. Phase 3**

Fall straight backward, pitching your opponent over you and causing him to land on his shoulders beyond you. When it is necessary to make a savage defence straighten your assaulting leg somewhat at the moment of the throw, and kick your victim in the private parts. This latter move in the trick is never resorted to except in case of apparent necessity.

**No. 267. Trick 43. Phase 4**

If you get your victim on his head, but find yourself unable to send him over your head to a fall on his shoulders, kick him on the leg that is in the air with one of your own legs, and send him over at your side.

No. 268. Trick 43. Phase 5

All through this trick you are supposed to have kept your assailant's arms pinned at your sides, just as the trick was begun in
Phase 1. When you have thrown your man sideways you will land
upon him in this position. His arms are pinned by the clutch that
you took in Phase 1. You now draw your elbows as close to each
other as you can, and as close as possible to your own body. This
arm-breaking pressure upon your victim's arms forces him to
surrender.

No. 269. Trick 44. Phase 1

The hold shown here is known to American wrestlers as the "Nelson." *Jiu-jitsu* men regard it as a very foolish hold to take. Your assailant, standing at your rear, throws both of his arms under yours, between your elbows and your shoulders, and then clasps his hands at the back of your neck. By applying severe pressure against the back of your neck he is able to force your head down; by throwing his elbows out sideways he can force your arms up higher. When seized in this hold throw your arms out horizontally sideways.

No. 270.  Trick 44.  Phase 2

Bend, and throw your left leg back between your adversary's legs.
This sudden move deprives your antagonist of the power to force
your arms up.   Swiftly seize one of your own wrists with your other
hand.

**No. 271. Trick 44. Phase 3**

If necessary, wrap your left leg around your opponent's left leg, and drag his leg up from the ground. Now, you have your man off his balance.

No. 272. Trick 44. Phase 4

Throw yourself to the right, carrying your man down as shown in illustration 272. Land with your victim underneath.

Trick 44.  Phase 5

Here the relative positions of the antagonists are shown at the instant of the fall.  Note that neither has changed the position of his hands.

Trick 44.  Phase 6

Swing over to the position shown in illustration No. 274, releasing your hold on your victim's left arm.  With your left hand seize your victim's right wrist, bending it backward across your right leg.  Increase the pressure by seizing your left wrist with your own right hand.  If necessary, make the pressure on your victim's captured arm more tormenting by pressing down upon his right hand with your left leg.  This brings submission.

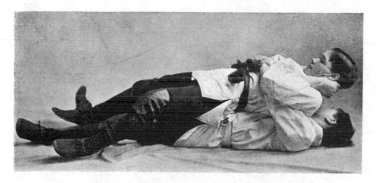

No. 273. Trick 44. Phase 5

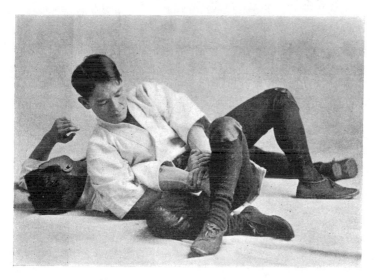

No. 274. Trick 44. Phase 6

No. 275. Trick 45. Phase 1

The possibility of applying this trick was shown in the First Section.  Here your opponent has his left hand on your right wrist, and his right hand at your right elbow.  With his right foot he kicks against the back of your right foot, sending your leg from under you and throwing you.

**No. 276.  Trick 45.  Phase 2**

Do not resist, but allow your adversary to throw you.  In going down twist out at his right, as shown in illustration No. 276, and with your left hand seize him at the back of his left knee.

**No. 277. Trick 45. Phase 3**

This attack throws your opponent off his balance, and he is obliged to release his left hand in order to save himself. Now clasp both your hands behind his left knee. Your right foot is outside your adversary's right foot.

**No. 278.   Trick 45.   Phase 4**

Holding the weight of your opponent's body on your back, rise and bend backward, at the same time forcing his captured left knee up in the air.   Fall backward, throwing your man.

### Trick 45.   Phase 5

Illustration No. 279 shows the relative positions of the contestants at the moment of the fall.   If necessary, wrap your right leg around your adversary's right leg.   Squeeze his captured left leg as close to your body as you can, digging the point of your left elbow in your victim's stomach.

### Trick 45.   Phase 6

Your victim has taken the only hold that presented itself.   With his left hand he has seized the back of your coat collar, and his right hand has seized your belt or the side of your coat.   It is his intention to throw you over to the right.   Go the way your victim wishes to throw you, but with your right hand reach up to your collar and seize his left wrist.   With your left hand seize your opponent's right wrist, and bend his arm backward over your right leg.   Throw your left leg over his captured fist in order to add to the arm-breaking pressure.

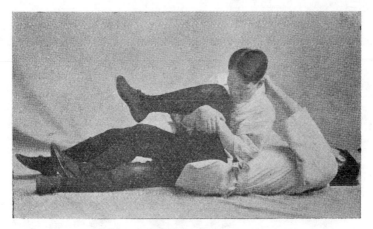

No. 279. Trick 45. Phase 5

No. 280. Trick 45. Phase 6

**No. 281. Trick 46. Phase 1**

At the beginning of this trick you have seized your opponent's left
wrist with both your hands, and have forced his left arm over your
shoulder, bending it down backward at the elbow. At the same
time bend forward as if to throw your adversary over your shoulder.
But this move is intended only to deceive your antagonist. He
drags back with his captured hand, and with his right hand seizes
your right elbow underneath, at the same time throwing his right
leg back of your right leg. He is now in position to throw you
backward to a dangerous fall.

**No. 282. Trick 46. Phase 2**

Astonish your adversary by yielding and by throwing a swift
somersault backward.

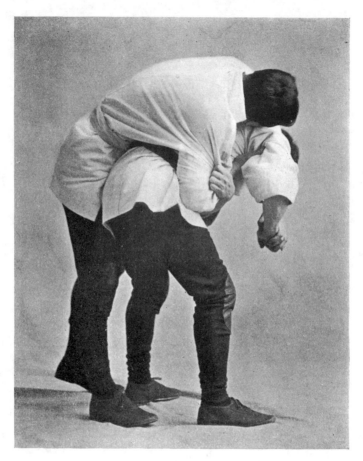

No. 283. Trick 46. Phase 3

The somersault brings yourself and your opponent up to standing position again, as shown in illustration No. 283. While this performance has a difficult look, it is an easy one for any trained gymnast.

No. 284. Trick 46. Phase 4

Your right hand is idle at this point, but awaiting future use. Your left hand clutches tightly at your opponent's right elbow.

**No. 285. Trick 46. Phase 5**

Now, with your right hand grab your adversary's right wrist. Go down swiftly to your right knee, extending your left leg.

No. 286. Trick 46. Phase 6

Phase 6.   Throw your victim over your right shoulder and fall
on him.   The relative positions are shown in illustration No. 286.
Catch your adversary's left wrist with your right hand.

Phase 7.   (See illustration for Trick 45, Phase 6.)   With your left
hand seize your opponent's right wrist, and bend his arm backward
over your right leg, aiding in this pressure by throwing your left
knee over his right fist.

No. 287. Trick 47. Phase 1

Sometimes, when you are thrown as shown in illustration No. 287, your opponent throws his body against your legs before they have had time to drop. Thus he wedges your legs in the air. At the same time, with his left hand he seizes your right wrist, and with his right hand your right elbow. He is now in a position to twist your captured elbow around toward your face, breaking your arm. Your defence against this trick begins by reaching over with your left hand and pressing the first two fingers against the top of his jaw-bone, just under the ear. There is a sensitive nerve here, pressure on which causes torment. With this pressure force your assailant to go over sideways.

**No. 288.  Trick 47.  Phase 2**

At the instant that your opponent goes over to the side rest your left hand on the floor and quickly turn a somersault.

**No. 289. Trick 47. Phase 3**

You will come to the position indicated by the man in the black belt. Your assailant's right hand is still clutching at your right elbow. With your left hand hold his right wrist. Now employ Trick 27, Phase 2.

**No. 290. Trick 48. Phase 1**

Here your opponent is shown employing a clever throw against you. As you reach for his lapel with your right hand he seizes your right wrist with his left hand, and throws his right arm over your right arm at the elbow. Now, with his left hand he forces your right fist up into the air and over, dragging your captured elbow toward him so that its point rests against his chest. Holding your elbow thus, he forces your right hand over your shoulder, at the same time stepping his right leg back of your right leg. Now he throws you backward, and ought to be able to make both your shoulders touch.

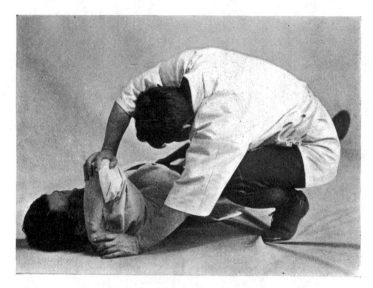

**No. 291. Trick 48. Phase 2**

Here your opponent is shown twisting your elbow around over your face in order to force your shoulder to the ground. With whichever foot or knee it is most convenient press severely against the right side of his abdomen.

No. 292.  Trick 48.  Phase 3

Quickly push your opponent's right elbow with your left hand.

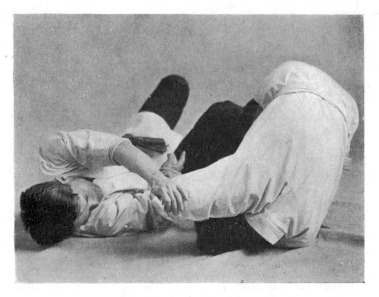

**No. 293. Trick 48. Phase 4**

Still pressing on your assailant's elbow, wriggle out from under him to your left.

No. 294. Trick 48. Phase 5

Leap upon your antagonist as shown in illustration No. 294, with your left knee pressing on his upper arm. With your right hand seize his right fingers, flexing them over upon his wrist and forcing him to submission.

**No. 295. Trick 49. Phase 1**

The start is made by your opponent seizing your right lapel with his right hand.

No. 296.  Trick 49.  Phase 2

If necessary, make your opponent release his grip by twisting and taking off his thumb, as explained in earlier tricks.  Advance your right foot just inside your adversary's right foot.

**No. 297. Trick 49. Phase 3**

Your right hand was employed in breaking the grip of your antagonist's right hand. Now, with your thumb wrapped around his thumb, and your finger tips pressing against the base of his thumb joint, force your adversary's right hand back toward his shoulder, as shown in illustration No. 297. While doing so, substitute your left hand for your right hand in the hold on his right thumb. As you make the change bring your right forearm smartly down on the inside of his elbow to assist in doubling up his captured right arm.

# Kano Jiu-Jitsu

No. 298. Trick 49. Phase 4

Now that you have forced your assailant's right hand back over his shoulder, change the hold on his thumb for one on his wrist, as shown in illustration No. 298. Your right hand seizes your own left elbow. With the back of your right leg " kick " the back of your antagonist's right knee, thus throwing him. Fall with your victim.

## Trick 49.   Phase 5

In the position shown in illustration No. 299 twist your opponent's captured right hand around to the outside.   With your left arm, and with added pressure from the left shoulder, force your victim's captured right elbow over across his chest.   At the same time your right knee is pressing forcibly into the soft flesh at your victim's right side.   Your victim may attempt to escape by rolling over to his left with you.   Therefore it is necessary to hold the back of his captured right hand firmly against the floor, and to flex his fingers forcefully over upon the wrist.   You will be obliged to inflict considerable pain upon your opponent in order to insure your own safety.

## Trick 49.   Phase 6

Now comes the torment that causes the submission to be quickly made.   Your right hand grasps your victim's captured right wrist, while your left hand envelops the back of his captured hand, bending his fingers over upon his wrist.   Your right knee is now pressing in the victim's stomach and your right forearm is forcing his captured right arm over against his face.

No. 299. Trick 49. Phase 5

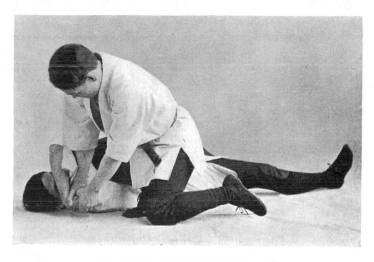

No. 300. Trick 49. Phase 6

**No. 301. Trick 50. Phase 1**

When your opponent takes this hold from the rear, without pinning your arms, he brings his own body as close to yours as he can.

No. 302.  Trick 50.  Phase 2

With your left hand seize his right thumb, pressing it backward, with your fingers at the base of his thumb joint, as described in some of the earlier tricks.

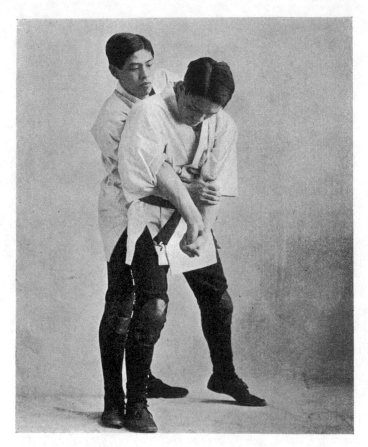

**No. 303. Trick 50. Phase 3**

Throw your right arm over your assailant's right arm, and seize your own left elbow. With your hold on your adversary's right thumb forcefully extend his right arm, as shown in illustration No. 303.

No. 304. Trick 50. Phase 4

Bend forward, as shown above, holding your arms down and as rigid as possible.

No. 305. Trick 50. Phase 5

Thrusting your right foot outside of your opponent's right foot and your left foot between his two feet, bend obliquely forward to the right and throw him over your shoulder. Secure his submission by any of the earlier tricks of this Section.

# SECTION III

No. 306.  Trick 1.  Phase 1

An opponent may seize one of your wrists, as shown in illustration No. 306.

**No. 3O7. Trick 1. Phase 2**

Flex your captured arm, the thumb side of your fist uppermost, as shown in illustration No. 307

**No. 308. Trick 1. Phase 3**

As in this position your antagonist holds your wrist only by the pressure of his thumb, it is easy to wrench your hand away from him. But, in starting this trick, the thumb side of your hand must always be uppermost.

No. 309.  Trick 2.  Phase 1

It may be that your opponent seizes one of your wrists with both of his hands.

No. 310.  Trick 2.  Phase 2

If you are not strong enough to wrench your captured wrist away from both of your opponent's hands by the use of the preceding trick, then it will be necessary to employ both of your own hands. Suppose it is your right wrist that has been seized.  Reach over with your left hand, with your left palm over the end of your right fist, and your left fingers under your right fist, as shown in illustration No. 310.

No. 311. Trick 2. Phase 3

Now, with the aid of your left hand, simply pull your right fist smartly up to your shoulder. The thumb side of the right fist must be uppermost when flexing your arm upward.

# Kano Jiu-Jitsu

**No. 312. Trick 2. Phase 4**

Pull your right fist up smartly toward your shoulder, as shown above, and the hold is broken.

Note.—If your assailant is a very strong man, and there is difficulty in flexing your arm, first bend your shoulder over a little toward your wrist, and the flexion becomes easier.

No. 313.  Trick 3.  Phase 1

Sometimes your assailant will seize both your wrists, as shown in illustration No. 313.

**No. 314.   Trick 3.   Phase 2**

Extend your arms straight down before you, and bend, pushing your fists down.

**No. 315.  Trick 3.  Phase 3**

This forces your assailant to bend his wrists and this weakens his hold.  Twist your fists to the outside, and flex your arms, with the thumb sides of your fists uppermost, as in Trick 1.

**No. 316.  Trick 3.  Phase 4**

Now, with a twist, and flexing your forearms, wrench free.

**No. 317.  Trick 3.  Phase 5**

In case you wish to follow up by seizing your antagonist's wrists, do not bring your hands up too high in flexing your arms, but make a twist and, as you wrench your own wrists free, clench your hands around your adversary's wrists.  At the time of seizing your antagonist's hands you will have opportunity, if you desire, to seize your adversary by a thumb or finger and to twist that member.

# Kano Jiu-Jitsu

No. 318. Trick 4. Phase 1

Here the assailant seizes you by the coat edge with his right hand. In this case, you must seize his thumb in the way that is now to be explained. The method must be studied carefully and mastered. Your assailant's thumb is to be flexed until it is doubled over upon itself. This pressure is applied at the very tip of the thumb-nail, so as to double the thumb up. If the pressure be applied farther up on the thumb-nail, the same amount of pain cannot be caused. (It is possible to get the idea of this tip-of-the-nail pressure in another way. Close your left hand. Now, with your right hand press against the extreme tip of the nail of the little finger, in an effort to force the little finger to close still more. The trick of this pressure on the nail must be mastered, as it is of great importance throughout the practice of *jiu-jitsu.*)

No. 319.  Trick 4.  Phase 2

As you take the seizure described in the foregoing, dig the ball
of your left thumb into the back of your assailant's right hand,
and, at the moment of forcing him to release his hand, be ready to
seize the third and fourth fingers of his hand, pushing them away
from the other fingers.

# Kano Jiu-Jitsu

No. 320. Trick 4. Phase 3

In the illustration above, still another way is shown of " taking off " the assailant's hand. If he seizes your coat edge with his right hand, press the ball of your left thumb against the ball of his right thumb. Wrap the fingers of your right hand around his captured thumb. Now push back his captured thumb with your left thumb, at the same time taking hold of his hand with your right hand, so that you can transfer the clutch from your left to your right hand. As shown in illustration No. 320, the transfer has been made. Now, with your left thumb, press against the nail tips of the last two fingers of your adversary's right hand, as described in the foregoing. This leaves your victim at your mercy. Should he attempt to reach you with his idle left hand, you can kick him in the abdomen and end the contest.

**No. 321. Trick 4. Phase 4**

If you wish to throw your adversary to his right, bend his right thumb over backward with your left thumb, as shown in the illustration. With your right thumb press against the back of his captured hand, thus doubling his hand up.

No. 322. Trick 4. Phase 5

If your opponent is very strong, quickly apply your left hand just as you have done with your right, as shown in illustration No. 322, and by twisting his hand well over to the right, throw your victim. If necessary, wedge your right foot just outside his right foot to aid in the throwing.

**No. 323. Trick 5. Phase 1**

Take off your assailant's attacking hand in the manner already explained, one of your hands forcing his thumb backward, and the other hand applying the finger-tip pressure to the last two fingers of his attacking hand.

No. 324. Trick 5. Phase 2

Take off the attacking hand and come to the position shown in illustration No. 324.

**No. 325. Trick 5. Phase 3**

Retaining the hold on your adversary's captured hand, swing quickly in front of your opponent.

No. 326.  Trick 5.  Phase 4

Go back of your victim with a wrench, placing your feet as shown
in illustration No. 326.

**No. 327. Trick 5. Phase 5**

If your opponent continues to resist, quickly drag his captured arm back, step with your left foot against the back of his upper arm, and throw him.

No. 328.  Trick 6.  Phase 1

This time your assailant has concluded to seize your coat edge with the back of his hand uppermost.

No. 329. Trick 6. Phase 2

With your thumbs pressing severely against the back of your opponent's assaulting hand, just between the bases of the two middle fingers, wrap your fingers around the under side of his hand.

**No. 330. Trick 6. Phase 3**

Press your adversary's captured hand hard, at the same time forcing downward, and thus take the hand off.

**No. 331. Trick 6. Phase 4**

Catch two of your adversary's fingers with each of your hands pulling his two pairs of fingers away, as if trying to tear his hand in two.

No. 332. Trick 6. Phase 5

Quickly turn your back upon your victim, but do not attempt to twist his elbow.

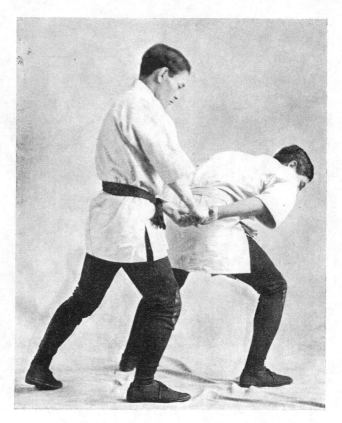

**No. 333.   Trick 6.   Phase 6**

Spring back of your victim, as shown in illustration No. 333.   If your victim still resists, place your right foot outside his left foot, and throw him to his left.   This throw will break his captured right arm.

No. 334. Trick 7. Phase 1

Here your assailant seizes your lapels or coat edge in any one of the numerous holds possible.

**No. 335. Trick 7. Phase 2**

Take off your assailant's hand by securing the hold on his thumb that has been explained already. Twist his thumb, and with your other hand take hold of his hand or wrist. All that is needed in this phase of the trick is to get your opponent's hand away from your coat.

**No. 336.  Trick 7.  Phase 3**

Just as your adversary is yielding his hold on your coat shift your own hands, and with your left seize his assaulting thumb. Now your right hand can be employed in taking away any hold that you prefer on his hand.

**No. 337. Trick 7. Phase 4**

If you wish, you can flex your adversary's hand upon his wrist, while twisting his thumb, in the manner shown in the illustration above. At the same time bring the point of your left foot forcefully into your victim's abdomen—and he is out of the contest!

**No. 338. Trick 7. Phase 5**

Instead of kicking, however, you may follow up the trick by
hauling your antagonist's arm over your shoulder, and throwing
him by the American trick known as the " flying mare." (This
" flying mare " feat has been explained in connection with preceding tricks.) In the " flying mare " the palm of the hand is down.
If it is wished to make your opponent's defeat more painful, carry
his arm over your shoulder with his palm uppermost, so that any
pull on his arm will force it to " bend the wrong way," thus making
the breaking of his arm possible.

## Trick 7

Phase 6. (No illustration.) Unless you intend to make the throw in earnest, it is unimportant whether you have the palm of your victim's captured hand turned up or down. In either case you make the feint of throwing him over your shoulder, and your antagonist naturally resists the effort to throw him. As he draws his arm back, he will throw his free arm around your neck with the intention of throwing you backward. Do not resist this move, but sink swiftly to your right knee, making sure to land behind your opponent. Now, twist his thumb and flex his hand, and your helpless victim will be very glad to surrender. Should you wish to throw your victim now, any one of several tricks described in the first part of the Second Section may be employed.

**No. 339. Trick 8. Phase 1**

When your opponent seizes you at your coat lapel or coat edge, employ the same " take-off " trick to get possession of the thumb, but in this trick do not break his hold on your coat. All that is needed is to get the twisting hold on his thumb.

**No. 340. Trick 8. Phase 2**

Come to the position shown in illustration No. 340, with your extended right leg against your opponent's left shin. In taking this position pull your adversary's captured hand violently toward you, and with your free hand seize his captured arm just back of the elbow, as shown.

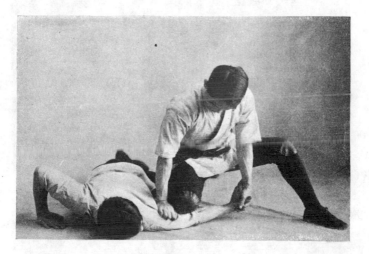

No. 341  Trick 8.  Phase 3

Throw your victim forward over your extended leg to the position shown above, and bring your right knee down on the back of his upper arm.  With knee and right hand push his shoulder down; and, with your left hand at his captured hand, force the latter up. If this upward pressure be forceful enough, it will break your victim's thumb and arm.

**No. 342. Trick 9. Phase 1**

Should your opponent, while at one side of you, instead of in front of you, seize you by the coat edge, break off his hold as has been already explained, and with your other hand seize his sleeve, as shown in illustration No. 342. (It has been explained in the descriptions of other tricks that it matters not whether your opponent wears sleeves of elbow length or of full length. The hold on his sleeve is taken just the same in either case.)

**No. 343.   Trick 9.   Phase 2**

Instantly pin your opponent's nearer foot with your own
nearer foot.   Then take his hand off your coat.   Pull his arm
forcefully across before your body, aiding this move by pushing
on his captured elbow.

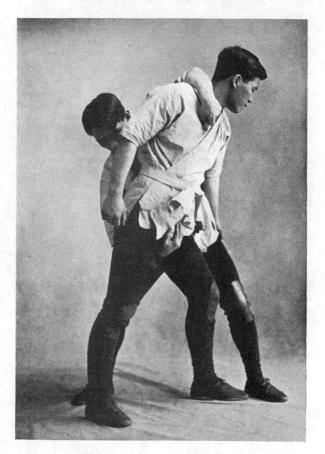

**No. 344. Trick 9. Phase 3**

As you get your adversary in front of you, throw your left arm around his neck, as shown in illustration No. 344, and slip your right arm under his crotch, taking hold on the cloth in front. The trick may stop at this point if you force your victim's head forward with your left arm, at the same time drawing backward and up with your right arm. This latter move results in an excruciating pressure that can be carried to such an extent as to make your victim faint.

No. 345. Trick 9. Phase 4

In a friendly wrestling match, the hold at the cloth in front of the crotch is shifted to one on the inside of the thigh, as shown in illustration No. 345. But in serious, dangerous combat the original hold is kept, and the victim's private parts are severely crushed as his head is forced down and his body pulled up.

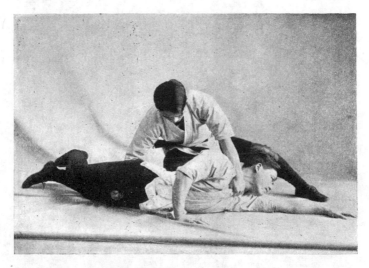

No. 346. Trick 9. Phase 5

As you throw your victim, he naturally will resist, so that the fall will be accomplished as shown in illustration No. 346. With your left hand seize the victim's coat in front of his " Adam's apple " and pull back across his right jugular, choking him. Your right hand is still at the cloth in front of his crotch, and you can draw back with this right arm, increasing the pressure, which may be made still more excruciating if you extend your right arm so that you can seize and hold his right wrist. Your right knee presses hard at the top of the victim's hip bone, increasing the torment.

**No. 347. Trick 10. Phase 1**

When you take off your assailant's left hand from your coat, your right hand is wrapped around his right thumb. Your left hand seizes his right hand at the back.

No. 348. Trick 10. Phase 2

Give a quick, wrenching twist, so that your adversary's captured hand is turned around. Now, quickly shift your hands, so that your left hand is wrapped around his thumb and your right hand has hold at the back of his captured hand. While twisting, give a vigorous pull at your victim's captured arm, and plant your left foot squarely against the back of his upper arm.

No. 349.  Trick 10.  Phase 3

When your victim attempts to get away from you by doubling his captured arm, allow him to bend his arm and go quickly back of him, taking the position shown in illustration No. 349, and continue the twisting of his hand.

**No. 350. Trick 10. Phase 4**

Throw your right arm around your victim's neck, seizing his left lapel and administering a severe choking against his "Adam's apple." Retain the original hold with the left hand, and bring your knee up against the captured forearm. Your victim is now obliged to surrender. This style of feat is known as a "standing submission," as contrasted with one in which it is necessary to throw your victim before securing victory.

No. 351.   Trick 11.   Phase 1

Here the " take-off " of the assailant's thumb is accomplished in
the usual way.   With your other hand seize your adversary's assaulting arm by a grip underneath the elbow, your knuckles digging
strongly against his " funny bone."

No. 352.  Trick 11.  Phase 2

Push down your opponent's thumb and force up his elbow.

No. 353.  Trick 11.  Phase 3

As you twist your antagonist's hand, and it goes over, shift your hold upon his hand so that your fingers are wrapped around his hand at the little-finger side, and the point of your thumb is pressing in at the base of his thumb.

**No. 354. Trick 11. Phase 4**

Bring your right thigh into place in order to wedge your opponent's captured hand, and force your right leg against the back of his left calf. Bear down hard on his captured elbow. If you wish to carry the trick further, kick your adversary's left leg from under him, throwing him.

**No. 355. Trick 11. Phase 5**

In illustration No. 355 the positions of the contestants are shown at the moment of the accomplishment of the throw. Force your victim's shoulder to the ground, and with your right knee push against the back of his captured hand, compelling your victim's submission. Of course, the pressure of your knee against the back of your victim's hand can be carried so far that it will result in breaking his hand.

No. 356    Trick 12.    Phase 1

Here the assailant starts his attack by seizing his opponent's coat edge.

No. 357.  Trick 12.  Phase 2

The method of defence in this phase must be studied carefully. Both of your thumbs are made to dig into the back of your assailant's right hand, just below the bases of the two middle fingers. The fingers of your right hand press into the palm of your victim's right hand.  Press hard with your thumbs, and use your right fingers to aid in twisting your adversary's hand over to your left.

**No. 358. Trick 12. Phase 3**

Still pressing in hard with your thumbs, force your antagonist's hand upward and over back on his wrist. All the while you must keep his thumb imprisoned with your fingers.

No. 359.  Trick 12.  Phase 4

Press as hard as you can with your thumbs, forcing your opponent to keep his captured hand open.  Swiftly let go of his thumb, and wrap each of your hands around two of his open fingers.  Now, press your opponent's hand up again and over backward on his wrist.

### Trick 12. Phase 5

Still keeping this hold, and forcing your opponent to bend, raise your right foot to his left shoulder.

### Trick 12. Phase 6

Suddenly come down to your left knee, and, as you do so, throw your right foot quickly from its last position over to the outside of your opponent's right knee. Now, pull his captured hand toward you, and, wedging him with your right foot against his right knee, throw him over to your left in the position shown in illustration No. 361. Now, leap upon your fallen adversary, planting your right knee forcefully against his left jugular. You have retained your hold upon your opponent's left hand, and now, if he attempt to escape, you are able to force his captured hand far enough backward upon his wrist to result in breaking the wrist.

No. 360. Trick 12. Phase 5

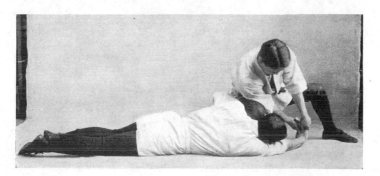

No. 361. Trick 12. Phase 6

No. 362.  Trick 13.  Phase 1

Every feature of this trick must be carefully mastered, as any deviation from the method renders the trick worthless.  In this phase seize your opponent with both your hands clasped at the back of his head.  He will think that you are trying to drag his head down forward, and he will resist.  Allow him to pull himself erect.

No. 363.  Trick 13.  Phase 2

But now you drag your antagonist's head down suddenly, and bring your right knee up smartly against his upper chest. Sometimes the knee is made to strike under the adversary's chin.

## Trick 13

**Phase 3.** (No illustration.) At this point there are two methods of making the throw. If your opponent has his right leg well in advance, then, just as soon as you have butted him in the chest with your knee, twist your body and suddenly throw your right leg back of his right leg at the outside, and throw your opponent over to his right. But, if your opponent has both his feet forward, at the instant after you bring your knee against his chest swing your foot—which is just in position—against your victim's crotch, striking him in the testicles. Now, with your knee still against your adversary's chest, throw yourself backward and throw your antagonist over your head. In making this throw, with your right knee against your opponent's chest, you will have an opportunity, if you wish, to strike your right foot against the inside of his right knee at the instant of falling, and this will enable you to throw your opponent over to your own right side.

No. 364. Trick 14. Phase 1

Here your opponent has thrown both arms around you, clasping his hands at the small of your back. He intends to crush in your back and to throw you over backward. If your adversary is a powerful man, and skilled in wrestling, he will look for an easy victory. Yet this is one of the easiest of predicaments from which to extricate yourself.

No. 365. Trick 14. Phase 2

Instantly throw your arms around his neck, as shown in illustration No. 365, and at the same time spring up and wrap your legs around at his waist-line, using your legs to crush in his wind as much as possible. As soon as your hands are clasped behind your adversary's neck, press the heels of your hands against the base of his skull, return to your feet, and thrust your right leg back of his right leg, or your left leg back of his left leg, and throw him to the side thus indicated.

**No. 366.  Trick 15.  Phase 1**

If your opponent seizes your shoulder, take pains to seize his shoulder from the outside.

**No. 367.  Trick 15.  Phase 2**

With your right foot kick the back of your opponent's left knee.

**No. 368. Trick 15. Phase 3**

Throw yourself backward, with your left leg behind both your adversary's feet. Your right knee presses the side of his left knee, and your right foot presses the back of his right knee. Quickly raise your left hand from the floor, and with it seize his left sleeve at the elbow. Now, roll quickly over to the right, carrying your opponent over with you.

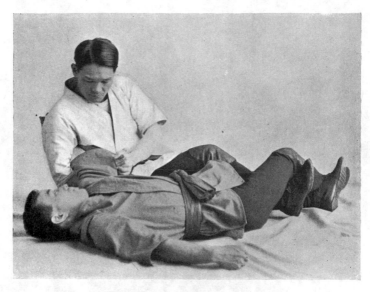

**No. 369. Trick 15. Phase 4**

As your man is thrown, rise to a sitting position, keeping your
legs in the same relative positions as when making the throw, as
shown in illustration No. 369.   Your right arm is still under your
victim's left arm, and his left hand is at your back.   With your left
hand clasp your own right hand and throw yourself violently back.
This, when done with force enough, will break your adversary's
arm.

**No. 370. Trick 16. Phase 1**

Here your assailant has seized at your left wrist with his left hand, and just below your elbow with his right hand, and has drawn your arm over his shoulder. Here he has you in what would seem to be a good position for making the throw.

**No. 371. Trick 16. Phase 2**

As your opponent attempts to throw you, do not resist, but seize his belt at the side, or push against the top of his hip bone. Allow your assailant to throw you over his shoulder, but come down on your feet at his right.

No. 372.   Trick 16.   Phase 3

With your right ha_d seize your adversary's right elbow firmly.

No. 373. Trick 16. Phase 4

Draw strongly with your captured left hand, and with your right hand push your opponent's right elbow up.

**No. 374. Trick 16. Phase 5**

Step back of your man, with your right foot between his two feet, and press your right hip against his right kidney. Pull his hand over backward with your left hand; with your right hand push his right elbow up and over backward. Now, throw your victim backward.

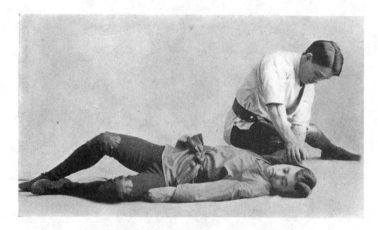

**No. 375. Trick 16. Phase 6**

Illustration No. 375 shows the relative positions of the combatants after the throw. Your right knee is pressing against your victim's upper arm. With your right hand force your victim's captured elbow over to the ground, while you twist his wrist and force submission.

**No. 376. Trick 17. Phase 1**

Here your opponent has seized you with both arms around your
waist. It is his intention to hug you to him, crushing in the small
of your back and throwing you.

[387]

**No. 377. Trick 17. Phase 2**

Throw both your arms around your adversary's neck, and leap up, throwing your legs around his body.

No. 378.  Trick 17.  Phase 3

If your opponent depresses the point of his chin, jab the point
of your right thumb against the top of his right jaw-bone, just
under the lobe of the ear, touching the sensitive nerve there and
forcing him to throw his head backward.  As soon as this advantage has been gained, with your hands crossed seize both lapels of
his coat.  One of your hands will be above the other.  Pull your
lower hand toward you, and with your upper hand push against
your opponent's " Adam's apple."  This chokes him so badly as to
shut off his breathing.

**No. 379. Trick 17. Phase 4**

Your opponent is obliged to throw back his head and to release his hold.

**No. 380. Trick 17. Phase 5**

Still retaining your strangle-hold, and applying it severely, drop
to your feet and thrust the back of your right leg against the outside of your opponent's right knee.  Now throw him.

**No. 381. Trick 17. Phase 6**

Fall with your right knee jabbing the soft part of your opponent's right side just over the hip-bone. Still keep the strangle-hold and force submission. If necessary, seize both lapels with your right hand, and twist the lapels closer together, all the while pulling one of the lapels toward you with your left hand.

No. 382.  Trick 18.  Phase 1

Here your opponent has seized one of your lapels with his right
hand.  Take off his thumb by pushing the ball of your thumb under
the ball of his thumb, and pressing your finger-tips in at the base
of his thumb.  (In case your assailant's thumb is wrapped tightly
into the cloth, it may be necessary to press the tip of your thumb
severely against the extreme end of his thumb-nail, doubling the
thumb up still more in this manner, until the pain causes your
adversary to release the hold with his thumb.)  With your left hand
seize your antagonist's elbow.

[393]

**No. 383.   Trick 18.   Phase 2**

Push your opponent's thumb over violently to his right, in order to force him to swing over to that side.   As he does so, seize his captured hand with both hands, digging both your thumb-tips into the back of his hand between the bases of his second and third fingers.   Flex his hand severely over upon his wrist.   He will try to strike you, but it is impossible for him to swing around so that he can employ his left hand.   As he attempts to do so, however, kick him in the abdomen.

No. 384.  Trick 18.  Phase 3

Now, swiftly drop to your left knee, twisting your adversary's captured hand quickly and violently over to his right, in order to guard against his left-hand blow, and at the same time thrust your extended right leg past his right leg, as shown in illustration No. 384. Throw your victim over your right leg.

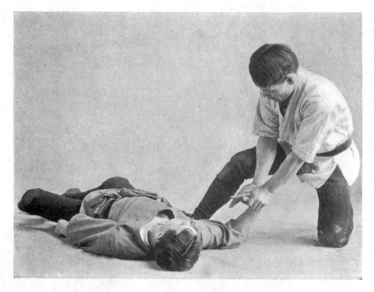

No. 385. Trick 18. Phase 4

Like a flash, before your opponent can have an opportunity to turn upon you, thrust your right heel against his right kidney, and wedge him with your foot against his side. At the same time continue flexing his captured hand severely over upon his wrist. This forces his submission.

**No. 386.  Trick 19.  Phase 1**

Here the assailant's hand has been taken off in practically the same manner as in the preceding trick.

No. 387.  Trick 19.  Phase 2

Yank up your opponent's captured elbow, at the same time twisting his thumb so that you can force his captured hand under his shoulder and push his hand behind him.  Now, still holding his thumb with your right hand, wrap the fingers of your left hand around the fingers of his captured right hand.  Hooking your own right foot around his right foot, throw yourself over backward to the ground, dragging your opponent with you and throwing him past your right shoulder.  This throw will result in breaking his right arm.

No. 388. Trick 19. Phase 3

There is another way of forcing a fall in this trick, and that is to pass your right leg back of your adversary's right leg, and to throw your right arm around his neck or chest, then forcing him over backward. But, if your opponent is a *jiu-jitsu* man, this is a very foolish trick to attempt. He will seize your right hand, bend forward, and swing around, facing the same way that you are facing, and will easily throw you. Hence, in this trick, you should never throw an arm around to your opponent's front

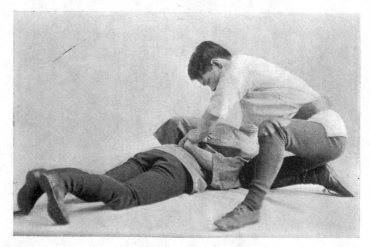

No. 389.  Trick 19.  Phase 4

The instant your man lands, as described in Phase 2, wedge your right knee against his right elbow to keep it pinioned, and continue twisting his captured thumb.   Throw your right arm around the back of his neck, seizing his right lapel and choking him into submission.

No. 390. Trick 20. Phase 1

The caution has been offered that, when you get an opponent's right hand behind his back, in the manner described in the preceding trick, you must not throw your right arm around the front of his neck. But you may, as shown here, throw your right arm around the *back* of his neck. Holding your adversary in this manner, kick his right side with your right knee, following this up instantly by throwing him to his own right.

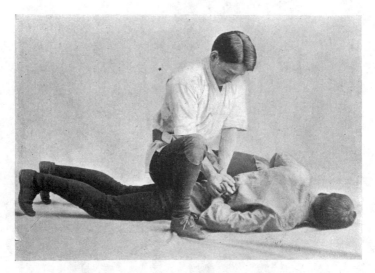

**No. 391. Trick 20. Phase 2**

Your adversary is thrown as shown in illustration No. 391. Instantly throw yourself astride of his back, with your left knee pressing hard at the base of his left shoulder-blade. Continue the twisting of your victim's captured wrist.

No. 392. Trick 20. Phase 3

Now, if you wish, you can secure a very simple lock by pressing your lower left leg against your victim's captured arm, between his elbow and his body. Now, by pressing your leg strongly against his wedged arm, you are able to break that arm.

**No. 393.  Trick 21.  Phase 1**

Here your opponent has seized your lapel with his left hand. Take off his hand by pressing the ball of your left thumb against the outer edge of his thumb near its tip, at the same time wrapping your fingers around the back of his hand.   Thu3 get your thumb around his thumb, and wrench his hand violently over to his own left as soon as your right hand has secured a hold at his left elbow.

[404]

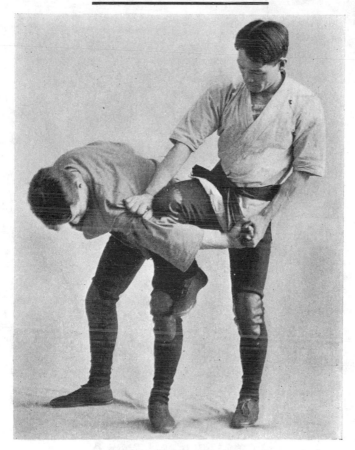

No. 394.   Trick 21.   Phase 2

This phase must be very carefully studied in its every detail.   Lifting up your opponent's left elbow, and twisting his thumb, swing around to his left until you are at his side and facing in the same direction that he does.   Turning the back of his captured left hand up, let go of his thumb and wrap your left hand around his left fingers so that a severely painful pressure may be applied to his little finger in the squeeze.   At the same time kick the outside of your opponent's left knee with your right foot and drag his captured hand toward you   This forces your antagonist to bend over to the right.   As he does so, instantly bring your knee up against the back of his arm.   Now, by bringing your victim's hand up and pressing downward with your knee, you are able to break your victim's arm.

[405]

No. 395. Trick 21. Phase 3

Instead of breaking your opponent's captured arm, you may, if you prefer, press steadily with your knee until you force your man over to the position shown above. Just as your adversary's head touches the ground, leap over to his right side, still retaining your twisting hold on his left hand. Thus you are able to force him over on to both shoulders.

Phase 4. (No illustration.) Instead of turning your victim over as in Phase 3, while twisting his captured left hand with your left hand, throw your right arm around his neck, and sit down, dragging him over backward with you. Throw your legs over his arms, and then apply both your hands in choking him.

No. 396. Trick 22. Phase 1

Here your opponent has taken a boxing attitude and means to strike you.

No. 397.  Trick 22.  Phase 2

Fend your opponent's assaulting left arm with your right forearm, as shown in illustration No. 397.

No. 398. Trick 22. Phase 3

As your opponent follows with his right fist, fend his right arm, as shown in illustration No. 398, and with your left foot give a severe kick at the side of his left shin or knee. This will stop the fight!

**No. 399. Trick 23. Phase 1**

When your opponent leads with his left fist, seize his left wrist with your right hand. The ability to do this unerringly can be acquired by practice. At the instant of doing this, with your right foot kick his left thigh and side, as shown in illustration No. 399.

**No. 400. Trick 24. Phase 1**

This trick is easily learned, and its performance astounds your assailant. The trick, however, is full of danger to your victim. Just as he leads for you with either fist, throw yourself down upon one side, as shown in the illustration above. Land your uppermost foot against your victim's knee or shin, and hook your lowermost foot behind his ankle. Push severely with your uppermost foot and pull your lowermost foot smartly toward yourself. Your opponent will probably receive a broken leg, and if he falls on the back of his head, a fractured skull will be added to his injuries.

[411]

**No. 401. Trick 25. Phase 1**

As your assailant throws his arms around your neck, with your right hand seize both his coat lapels. (Practice by the student at this work of lapel twisting should be very frequent and thorough.) With the back of your hand toward yourself, fold your thumb in one of your adversary's lapels. Fold the second finger of your same hand—and, if you wish, the third and fourth—in the other lapel of your antagonist. Your index finger goes between the two lapels. Take this hold close to the throat. Now, gather the cloth up as close as possible with your thumb and fingers. Twist your hand around in order to make the choking pressure more effective. The first phalange or knuckle of the thumb is generally applied, while twisting, to the " Adam's apple."

[412]

**No. 402. Trick 25. Phase 2**

With the lapel still retained, swing around quickly to your left, so as to present your left side to your opponent. As you do so, go down upon your right knee and extend your left leg past his left leg. With your hold on your adversary's lapel, bring him forcibly over your shoulders, while with your left hand seizing his left leg at the back of the knee. Note that in this attack your opponent's left breast is made to strike upon the back of your head.

**No. 403. Trick 25. Phase 3**

Bending to your right side, and extending your left leg still more rigidly, throw your opponent over your shoulders.

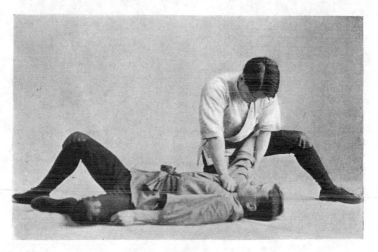

**No. 404. Trick 25. Phase 4**

Your victim will be thrown to the position shown in illustration
No. 404.

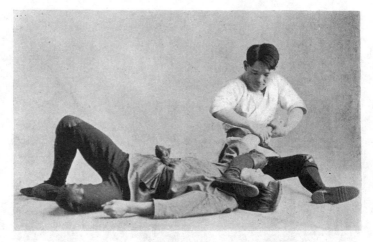

**No. 405. Trick 25. Phase 5**

Force your right leg under your victim's right arm, and with your foot force back his chin, so that you can apply a choking with your leg. Bend his right arm backward over your right leg to aid in forcing submission.

Note.—Unless a "knock-out" is desired, great care must be used in this trick. In Phase 2 it is possible to bring the nipple of your adversary's left breast sharply against the point of the back of your head, and this stops the action of the heart. This in reality kills the victim. Since the *jiu-jitsu* men are able, by the employment of *kuatsu*, or revivification, to bring back to life, Occidentals make the mistake, generally, of supposing that such an attack produces only insensibility. The services of a medical man not versed in *kuatsu*, however, would not result in restoring life.

**No. 406. Trick 26. Phase 1**

Here your opponent prepares to strike you. (The Japanese do not admire boxing, which explains the apparent inaccuracy of the positions in illustration No. 406. If an adversary reaches out with his left fist, a *jiu-jitsu* man responds by opposing his extended right fist. This enables one better to employ *jiu-jitsu* defence methods against the boxer.)

**No. 407.  Trick 26.  Phase 2**

At the instant that your assailant strikes out with his left fist, quickly swerve to his left, and with your right hand push his left elbow away.  If necessary, kick his abdomen with your left foot.

No. 408.   Trick 26.   Phase 3

Study phase 2 for a moment, and you will understand how it is easy to throw your left arm swiftly under your opponent's arm and around his neck at his right side.   As you do this you step behind your opponent at his left, and bend forward in order to bring his back over yours.   At the same instant your right hand seizes your adversary at the back of his left knee.

[419]

**No. 409. Trick 26. Phase 4**

Bend still farther forward, and hoist your victim across your back.

No. 410.   Trick 26.   Phase 5

As soon as you get your opponent across your back, let go with your right hand at his knee, and, with your left arm still around his neck, swing him around at your own left and drop him on the ground in front of you.   Study the positions of victor and victim in illustration No. 410.   You will note that the victor has his arms so placed around the victim that he can bear his head down hard on the victim's left shoulder, and, by hugging the victim's neck up to him, the victor is able to crush the neck.

Note.—Return to Phase 2 of this trick.   When kicking in the abdomen, if the assaulting heel lands near the navel, and the point of the foot strikes just over the victim's left nipple, this attack may be made to result fatally.   It should never be attempted in earnest by one who is not an expert at *kuatsu*.

**No. 411. Trick 27. Phase 1**

Guard against your enemy's left fist by parrying his blow with
your right forearm, as shown in illustration No. 411.

**No. 412.  Trick 27.  Phase 2**

When parrying any blow by your antagonist, close in quickly, in order to prevent him from striking a full-arm blow.

**No. 413. Trick 27. Phase 3**

At the same time that you put an adversary's arm down and close in, with the top of your head strike at the opponent's jawbone near the ear, or strike against the cheek-bone or just behind the temple. If an adversary, at the time of closing in with him, has his mouth slightly open, deliver a blow under or against the point of the jaw and follow this up instantly by striking with your head against the adversary's jaw-hinge. This will generally dislocate the victim's jaw.

[424]

No. 414.  Trick 28.  Phase 1

Here your opponent has taken a sleeve hold for wrestling.  He is pulling at your left arm, and pushing against your right arm. Bending your right elbow, seize your opponent's left sleeve, as shown in illustration No. 414.

**No. 415.   Trick 28.   Phase 2**

Push your antagonist's head over by forcing your open hand against his neck, and with the back of your left knee strike forcibly against the back of his left knee.   Quickly throw your man down backward.

Phase 3.   (No illustration.)   Just as you throw your victim over backward, swing around so that you can jump your right leg over his left arm.   As he lands upon his back, this will enable you to fall across his body, with your feet at his right.   Your head is off at his left, at right angles with his body, and you have his left arm seized with both your hands, forcing his captured arm to bend backward against your right leg.   Thus you are able to break your victim's arm if you wish. When this trick is employed deliberately for breaking an arm, it is broken at the instant that the victim strikes the ground.

**No. 416.  Trick 29.  Phase 1**

When your intended victim strikes at you with either of his fists, throw your own opposite fist up to counter, and at the same instant kick with the bottom of the foot corresponding with your employed arm against your opponent's groin.

**No. 417.  Trick 29.  Phase 2**

If you have employed your right hand and foot in the preceding phase, now fall instantly to your left side, bringing your right foot up strongly against your victim's scrotum.

**No. 418.  Trick 30.  Phase 1**

Here, as your opponent strikes at you with his left fist, duck and dodge quickly to your adversary's left, at the same time fending off his left elbow with a forceful blow from your open right hand.

No. 419. Trick 30. Phase 2

It is not really necessary to seize the adversary's left wrist, as shown in illustration No. 418. Your opponent, at the moment when you have fended off his left arm, is bending slightly forward on his left leg. Like a flash close in on him at his left, and make a quick jump, landing with the back of your left leg against the back of his left leg close to his thigh. Bend over enough so that with your right hand you can seize your opponent's left ankle. Yank his ankle up and sit down, pitching your opponent forward on his face.

**No. 420. Trick 31. Phase 1**

Your opponent has taken his position with his left fist forward, but you have confused him by bringing your right fist forward to oppose it. This forces your assailant to bring his right fist and right side forward, and he attempts to strike you with his right fist. As he does so, duck and spring nimbly to his right, catching the outside of his elbow and pushing his arm over toward his left. As your opponent cannot use his right arm effectively for the instant, he may attempt to swing around to his right again so that he can employ his left fist. As he does so, bring your left foot with a swinging kick against his abdomen.

**No. 421. Trick 31. Phase 2**

After having gripped your adversary's right elbow with your left hand, employ your right hand in seizing his right wrist. At the same time bring your left foot up in a kick against your opponent's right knee. This forces his knee to bend. Pull his arm toward you, and he is forced down in the manner depicted in illustration No. 421. Push your knee against the back of his right upper arm, and pull up at the wrist, breaking his arm.

**No. 422. Trick 32. Phase 1**

Here your opponent strikes with his right fist, and you counter with your own right fist, at the same time bringing around your right foot in a swinging kick and landing it in his right groin.

### Trick 32.   Phase 2

Just at the instant that your right foot lands, as in the preceding phase, throw yourself down as shown in illustration No. 423. Sometimes your opponent will help you by catching at your foot, but in any case you must go to the floor, with your right foot still against your opponent's right groin and your left foot kicking his left calf.   With both your hands seize your adversary's foot in the manner shown in the illustration.

### Trick 32.   Phase 3

Twisting your adversary's captured foot, press hard with your left foot against your opponent's left calf, and roll over to your own right.   You will bring down your opponent, as shown in illustration No. 424.

No. 423. Trick 32. Phase 2

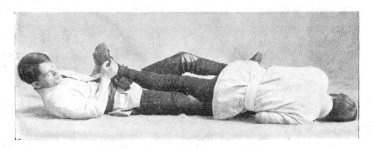

No. 424. Trick 32. Phase 3

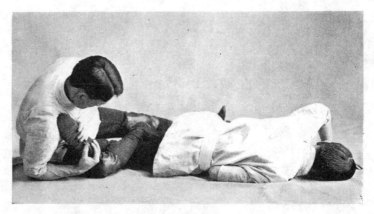

**No. 425. Trick 32. Phase 4**

Now, throw your right leg over your opponent's captured right leg, forcing your right foot between his thighs and digging the point of your foot against his scrotum. At the same time, press hard with your right shoulder against the outside of your victim's captured right foot, forcing the foot over and breaking his ankle.

**No. 426. Trick 33. Phase 1**

This illustrates any hold that your opponent takes from the rear with his arms under your arms and his hands clasping in front.

**No. 427.   Trick 33.   Phase 2**

First of all, you must take off your assailant's right hand.   Do this, when his fist is closed tightly, by wrapping the fingers of your right hand around his fingers, with your hand folded over his hand. With your finger-tips press with all your strength against the very tips of the balls of your adversary's third and fourth fingers, as if you were trying to close his fist even tighter.   This will cause your antagonist such pain that he will relax his grip, and you can force him to unclench his fingers.

No. 428.   Trick 33.   Phase 3

Pressing your elbows tightly to your sides, take off your assailant's right hand, seizing his first two fingers and twisting them over
to your right.   Now, in the same fashion, prepare to take off your
opponent's left hand.

No. 429.  Trick 33.  Phase 4

Extend your arms quickly to your sides and hold them there rigidly.  With the heels of your hands bear down upon the backs of your adversary's hands, and with your fingers twist his captured fingers upward.

**No. 430. Trick 33. Phase 5**

With your right arm still rigidly extended, bring your own left arm and your opponent's up over your head.

**No. 431. Trick 33. Phase 6**

Yank your victim's captured right hand strongly over to your
left side, and bring his left arm down forcefully over your right arm.
At the same instant kick his right foot from under him with your
right foot against his right heel, and throw him. Your victim is
likely to have broken fingers, broken wrists, and broken elbows.

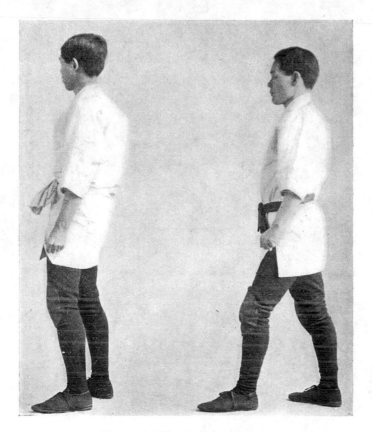

No. 432. Trick 34. Phase 1

This trick supplies the best method of stealing upon an adversary from the rear and throwing him.

No. 433.  Trick 34.  Phase 2

The safest way of seizing an intended victim around his neck from the rear has been explained in another trick.  It consists in wrapping the fingers of one of your hands around the fingers of your other hand, and folding each thumb in the palm of the other hand.  When you have taken this hold, bring one of your knees forcefully up in your victim's back, and with the toes of your foot kick your victim in the scrotum.  This kick is made possible, after your knee has landed hard in his back, by bending your opponent back and to one side, thus forcing him to spread his legs.

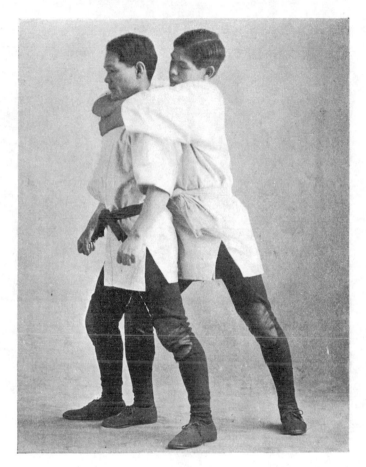

**No. 434. Trick 35. Phase 1**

Here your opponent has seized you with an unwise hold around your throat.   The first step in your defence must be to bring your chin down strongly, thus making it all but impossible for your adversary to use any strangling pressure.

No. 435. Trick 35. Phase 2

Seize at least two of the fingers of each of your assailant's hands. (The method of doing this has been explained in Trick 33.)

No. 436.  Trick 35.  Phase 3

Quickly yank your adversary's right hand around to your left side, and his left arm over your head to the right, at the same time swinging so as to press your left side against his abdomen.

No. 437. Trick 35. Phase 4

Bend swiftly forward, throwing your opponent over your back. Broken bones will result for your victim.

**No 438. Trick 36. Phase 1**

An assailant seizes you from behind, throwing his arms around your neck, as shown in illustration No. 438.

No. 439.  Trick 36.  Phase 2

If necessary, apply the pressure to the finger-tips that has been explained in other tricks in the foregoing.  Throw your hand that is still unemployed across your own chest and seize your opponent's elbow.

**No. 440. Trick 36. Phase 3**

Your assailant may try to drag you over backward. As he does
so, wrench his captured arm away from your neck, your fingers
being over the corresponding fingers of his captured hand. If it
is your opponent's left hand that you have, then kneel quickly at
his own left and on your own left knee. Bend his hand over backward upon his wrist and push up at the captured elbow. Then
quickly rise behind your adversary, now pushing down on his elbow
and bending his hand severely forward upon his wrist. (See illustration No. 440.) Now, forcing your victim to bend well forward,
use your right heel to kick his left shin hard, following this up instantly by throwing him.

[451]

No. 441.  Trick 37.  Phase 1

If you seize an adversary around his waist while standing at one side of him, his first move will be to throw his nearer arm around your neck, as shown in illustration No. 441.

No. 442. Trick 37. Phase 2

If you are at your adversary's right side, go down instantly to your right knee, at the same time thrusting your right arm under his right knee and yanking it up.

Trick 37.   Phase 3

Throw your opponent over to the position shown in illustration No. 443.   At once, with your right hand, seize your adversary's right hand, with your fingers over the back of his hand and squeezing his fingers together.   His hand should be held just in front of your own chin.

Trick 37.   Phase 4

Twisting your victim's right wrist, press your right knee hard against his right buttock.

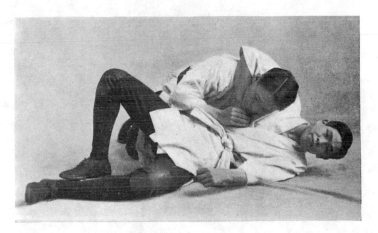

No. 443.  Trick 37.  Phase 3

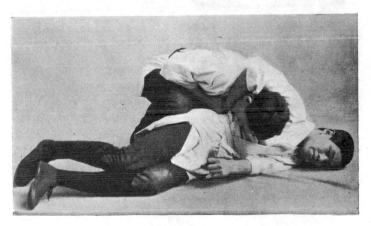

No. 444.  Trick 37.  Phase 4

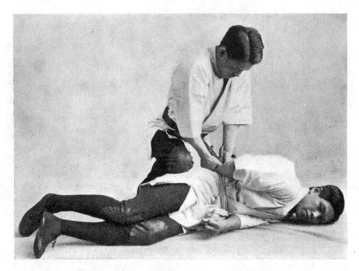

**No. 445.  Trick 37.  Phase 5**

Raise yourself up over your victim as shown in illustration No. 445.  Now employ both your hands upon your opponent's captured right hand.  Take such hold that your left thumb digs in at the base of his right thumb, and your right thumb presses against the middle of his wrist at the point where the latter joins the hand. With this hold, twist your victim's captured wrist over until he submits.  The twisting may be applied so severely as to break the wrist.

**No 446. Trick 38. Phase 1**

Your assailant may attempt to choke you by using any one of
the crossed hand holds described in the previous tricks.

**No. 447. Trick 38. Phase 2**

With your right hand seize your adversary's left elbow, thrusting your left forearm under his left forearm. This is assuming that his left hand is uppermost. In the elbow seizure, the thumb of your assaulting hand digs in severely against the inner side of the " funny " bone. Your left forearm, while under his left forearm, passes over his right forearm.

**No. 448.  Trick 38.  Phase 3**

Sometimes it will be sufficient to push your left hand against your adversary's left elbow, pushing against your own left hand with your right hand, and forcing your man over to a fall.  But when the elbow is seized with pressure against the " funny " bone, as described in the last phase, step quickly to your opponent's left while forcing his captured elbow up as shown in illustration No. 448.

**No. 449.   Trick 38.   Phase 4**

This must be practised with great caution.   With your own left hand flex your victim's captured left forward upon his wrist, at the same time forcing his captured hand back of him and twisting his elbow forward.   As your victim seizes your right knee, throw your left leg across his neck and squeeze his neck between your two knees.   Now, let go of his elbow, and with both of your hands carry his right hand up over your right shoulder.   Fall over backward, carrying your victim with you.   If great caution be not used, this will break your victim's neck.

No. 450. Trick 39. Phase 1

Sometimes when an adversary catches you in position at his side, with your head down, he thrusts his arms under your shoulders and clasps his hands high up on your back. This gives him, apparently, a great advantage.

**No. 451.  Trick 39.  Phase 2**

Hug your elbows as close to your body as you can, clasping your hands in front, if necessary, in order to aid in the severe straining pressure upon your assailant's arms.  At the same time throw your own head close to the ground and walk rapidly backward, keeping up the pressure with your own arms, so that your victim thinks that his arms are being broken.  The pain forces him to his knees, as shown in illustration No. 451.

No. 452. Trick 39. Phase 3

Just as your opponent touches his knees, seize his left elbow with both your hands, but do not relax the crushing pressure of your arms against his arms. Turn over to your own right, and this throws your opponent's right leg in the air, as shown in illustration No. 452.

**No 453. Trick 39. Phase 4**

Complete the throw to your own right by rolling over upon your victim, landing with your head on his abdomen. Grasp the fingers of his left hand by pairs, digging your thumbs into the back of his captured left hand. Now, using the soles of your feet in order to obtain a starting leverage, throw a somersault, landing on your knees at your victim's right side. This will bring you to the position shown in Trick 37, Phase 5. This trick results in a broken arm for the victim.

**No. 454. Trick 40. Phase 1**

Here is shown a favourite form of strangle-hold. With his left hand your assailant has seized your coat lapels, twisting them tightly together. With his right hand he has seized your right collar, pressing his right knuckles into your " Adam's apple " in order to choke you into submission.

No. 455.   Trick 40.   Phase 2

Clasp your hands, and force your arms between your assailant's arms.   Wedge your left elbow under his right forearm, and, with your hands still clasped, force your right forearm against his left wrist.

Phase 3.   (No illustration.)   Suddenly unclasp your hands, and throw your arms wide open.   This breaks your assailant's hold upon you.   As you break his hold, turn your back upon him and with your right hand seize his left wrist.   Throw your left arm over his captured left arm, your left hand coming under his left elbow.   Now complete your turn so that his legs are at the right side of your body.   Bend well forward and throw your victim over your back.

[466]

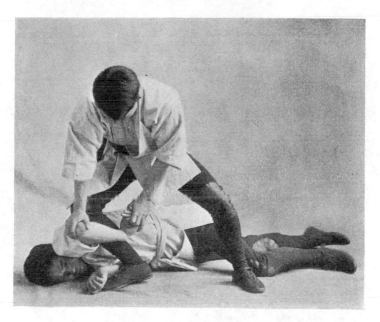

**No. 456. Trick 40. Phase 4**

Fall upon your victim in the manner shown in illustration No.
456. Wrapping your left hand around the back of his left hand,
twist it forcibly over to the little-finger side. Note the positions of
your other hand and of your two feet and right knee. Push hard
on your victim's left elbow and twist his captured hand over against
your right lower leg. If your victim does not quickly submit his
left arm and wrist will be badly broken.

No. 457. Trick 41. Phase 1

Here your opponent starts to run toward you. It may be his intention to strike you, or to seize you by the arms and attempt to throw you over. Study the exact position of the man (in the black belt) on the defensive. Study the positions of his feet, the looseness of his knees, and the way in which he holds his hands. His body is all but erect, yet not rigidly so. The man on the defensive has every muscle relaxed.

No. 458. Trick 41. Phase 2

Just as your opponent is to strike or seize you, and before he has opportunity so to do, go down upon one knee, putting the foot of the other leg forward. At the same time grasp your assailant's legs just back of the knees, as shown in illustration No. 458, and strike the top of your head severely into your adversary's private parts. If you strike effectively, the back of your head will touch the victim's abdomen.

**No. 459. Trick 41. Phase 3**

If the bout be a friendly one, this blow at the private parts is struck just the same, but not hard enough to cause injury. As soon as your head is at your opponent's crotch, push your head through between his legs, and rise, throwing him over your back, as shown in illustration No. 459.

Phase 4. (No illustration.) Your opponent, as he goes over your back, will throw one hand to the floor in an effort to save himself. In the illustration for the last phase it is his right hand that he has thrown to the floor. Without changing your own position, wrap your right leg around his right arm, and then swing quickly and strongly around to your own left. This strain will break your victim's arm. If he puts down his left arm, wrap your right leg instead around his left arm, but it will be necessary, in this case, to make the swing of your body around to your right.

# Kano Jiu-Jitsu

**No. 460. Trick 42. Phase 1**

Your assailant may seize you with his hands at the wrist and elbow of one of your arms, as shown in illustration No. 460, twisting your captured wrist and holding at the back of your elbow. As shown in the illustration, he has thrust his left leg between your two legs, with the side of his left knee pressing against the side of your left knee. This is a good lock to obtain preparatory to throwing you to your right.

[471]

No. 461.  Trick 42.  Phase 2

Swing quickly around to your own left, shifting your left leg to a position between your opponent's two legs.  At the same time wrap your left arm firmly around your assailant's left arm.

No. 462. Trick 42. Phase 3

Now throw yourself backward, as shown in illustration No. 462. In his fall your opponent is obliged to release his right-hand hold on your right wrist. Now, with your right hand still under you, seize his left wrist.

Phase 4. (No illustration.) Study the illustration for the preceding phase, and you will understand how, if you suddenly throw your feet in the air, and turn a back somersault, you will thereby break your victim's captured left arm.

No. 463.  Trick 43.  Phase 1

When you have thrown your adversary, and have fallen astride of him, as shown in illustration No. 463, he may reach up and seize your lapels, intending to choke you by means of any one of the strangle-holds already explained.  If he takes a lapel-hold with both hands, clasp your own hands as shown in the illustration.

**No. 464. Trick 43. Phase 2**

Thrust your clenched hands between your adversary's arms, and up toward your head, and the pressure of your arms against your opponent's arms will break his hold.

**No. 465. Trick 43. Phase 3**

Instantly seize your opponent's right wrist, bending his captured arm over your left upper leg. With your right hand seize his right lapel and dig your knuckles into either his " Adam's apple " or his right jugular vein. Continue the pressure on his captured arm, and also the choking, until your victim submits.

**No. 466.   Trick 44.   Phase 1**

Here your right hand grips your opponent's collar, while your left hand seizes his belt.

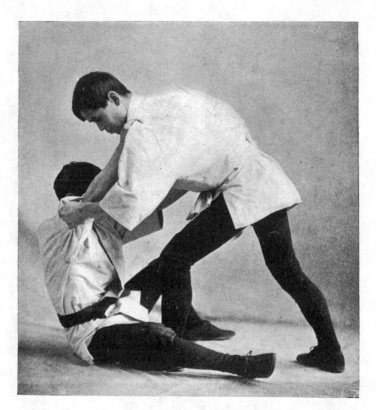

**No. 467. Trick 44. Phase 2**

Sit down quickly, and with your right calf hit your opponent's left ankle at the outside, as shown in illustration No. 467. At the same instant hit the inside of your adversary's left knee with your own left knee.

No. 468.   Trick 44.   Phase 3

Now, strike up with your left foot at your opponent's right thigh. At the moment of doing so, lean backward and pull your opponent over you.

Your opponent will fall over you in the manner shown in illustration No. 469. Your right leg is still wedging his left leg. With your left knee kick his right thigh just below the hip. Throw him over to his own right.

Phase 5. (No illustration.) As you go over your left arm is wrapped around your opponent's right arm, so that the back of his hand rests against your shoulder. This gives you an arm-breaking grip. As your victim lands upon the ground, throw your right foot over under his right shoulder, at the same time throwing your left foot around the left side of his neck. You now have a lock on your opponent from which he cannot escape, and you can force him to submission by the breaking pressure on his captured right arm.

No. 470.  Trick 45.  Phase 1

Here your opponent throws both arms around one of your knees, intending to throw you backward.  As he does so, throw one arm around his neck, as shown in illustration No. 470, and with your other hand seize his opposing elbow.

**No. 471. Trick 45. Phase 2**

Suddenly bring up your captured knee—a move which your
opponent is powerless to resist—and strike him in the abdomen.
Then throw your foot between his legs, your shin now striking him
in the lower abdomen. Then throw your foot between his legs,
your shin striking him smartly in the private parts.

No. 472. Trick 45. Phase 3

If, for any reason, you are unable to employ the preceding phase, leap up, throwing your right foot back of your opponent, as shown in illustration No. 472, and with your left foot kick him at the inside of his right calf.

**No. 473.  Trick 45.  Phase 4**

If the kick at your opponent's right calf be given hard enough, and if you hold on to his neck tightly, you will be able to throw yourself backward, with your right knee pressing in your adversary's abdomen.  Your victim is brought down standing on his head, and the relative positions of the contestants are shown in illustration No. 473.

No. 474. Trick 45. Phase 5

When you are unable to employ the preceding phase, then, instead, throw both your arms around your adversary's neck, and leap up, throwing your legs around his waist, with your feet crossed over his buttocks. Your opponent retaliates by falling forward, thus throwing you on your back. As you fall, press against your adversary's chin forcibly with your chest, with severe strain at the back of his neck, at the same time forcing your knee into your adversary's abdomen, and your victim is defeated.

No. 475.  Trick 46.  Phase 1

Here your opponent, attacking you from the rear, has secured a
hold that he thinks will be valuable to him.  With his right hand
he has seized your left elbow, and with his left hand your right elbow.
He intends to throw you forward at his left side.

[486]

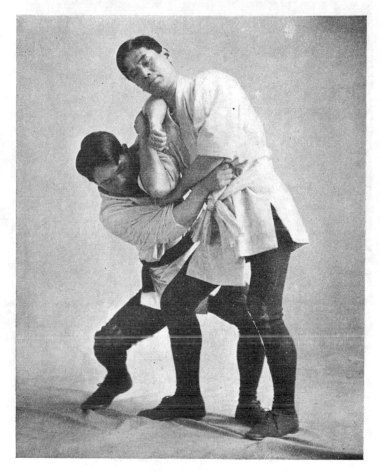

**No. 476.  Trick 46.  Phase 2**

Twist away from your adversary, getting to his right, and with your left leg behind his right leg.  Be careful to bend your knees just as is shown in illustration No. 476.

**No. 477.   Trick 46.   Phase 3**

Now you are in position to swing quickly around, facing your
opponent.   With your right hand seize his belt at his left side.
With your left hand seize his left lapel, and, pressing your wrist
against his " Adam's apple," administer a severe choking.   With
your right foot kick your opponent's left knee.   (Be careful to note
that your right leg is behind your adversary's right leg.)   Throw
yourself backward, dragging your opponent over with you.   For
compelling submission from your victim, employ any suitable trick
described in the beginning of the Second Section.

No. 478.   Trick 47.   Phase 1

Your opponent may leap and seize your belt at either side of your body.

No. 479.   Trick 47.   Phase 2

When this attack is made, cross your hands in front of your adversary's chest.   Your right hand seizes his right lapel, while your left hand seizes his left coat edge lower down than the lapel.   Pull his right lapel across and against his " Adam's apple," choking him, and pull his left coat edge obliquely to the right.   At the same time swing around to his right, throwing your left leg in front of his right leg, as shown in illustration No. 479.

No. 480.  Trick 47.  Phase 3

Swing around still more to the right, and with the back of your left calf strike smartly against your opponent's left knee.  As you do this, press your knuckles into your opponent's jugular.

**No. 481.  Trick 47.  Phase 4**

Now, throw your victim forward, causing him to land on his head and left elbow.  In this position wrap your left leg around your opponent's left forearm, and, with this hold, twist his arm until he submits.

# Kano Jiu-Jitsu

## Trick 48

Phase 1. (No illustration.) There is a favourite form of defence with American wrestlers against certain holds. This defence consists of throwing the right hand over the adversary's left shoulder, and seizing one's own right wrist with the left hand. The left forearm is now in position to be pushed against the adversary's neck, forcing him away. This style of defence is employed when an assailant secures a hold with both arms around the waist. A Japanese variation of this defence consists in taking the opponent's left lapel with the left hand, and the right coat edge with the right hand. Now, pulling down on the coat edge and across the throat with the lapel, the opponent is forced backward and made to break his hold. But the adept has a handy trick for meeting either of these defences. In the case of the Japanese hold, the man on the defensive breaks up the hold by taking off thumb or fingers of the assaulting left hand, as explained in earlier tricks. If the American form of the defence is employed against the man on the defensive, then the left hand is taken away by seizing your adversary's left hand with your own left hand and bending it over upon the back of his wrist. Now, throw your idle right arm over your adversary's captured left arm and make a turn, presenting your back to him, next bending well forward. Now, your adversary's captured left arm is over your back. Thrust your left foot out past and around his right foot and quickly sit down.

No. 482. Trick 48. Phase 2

If your adversary is experienced, or lucky, he will turn a somersault in going down, as, if he does not, his arm will be broken. If he makes the somersault, he will come to the position shown in illustration No. 482. As your opponent falls, fall with him, wedging his captured arm with your nearer knee and flexing his hand severely upon his wrist.

Trick 49

Phase 1. (No illustration.) Should your opponent take a hold with both arms around your waist and his hands clasped at your left side, quickly throw your right arm up in front of his neck, so that your hand passes down over his back. Get a good hold on any cloth there with your right hand. At the same time, with your left hand, take off whichever hand of your adversary is uppermost in his clutch. While doing this, wrap your right leg around your antagonist's left leg. Your right leg is now pressing against his private parts. Bend backward, and your adversary is compelled to bend with you. Releasing your right foot, kick at his left foot in order to compel him to fall, and, as he does so, wheel swiftly and throw your left leg around over his neck.

## Trick 49. Phase 2

Now, simply sit down and you will drag your opponent to the position shown in illustration No. 483.

## Trick 49. Phase 3

When you have your victim's neck well under control, bring your victim's captured hand up into the air, as shown in illustration No. 484, and twist his wrist and thumb until he submits. This move may be aided, of course, by strangling with your legs.

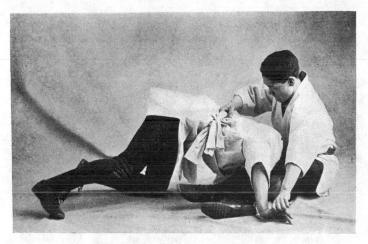

No. 483.   Trick 49.   Phase 2

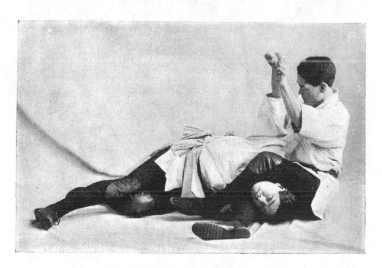

No. 484.   Trick 49.   Phase 3

**No. 485. Trick 49. Phase 4**

When you have the wrist twisting well applied, and the legs in good position for administering the choking, pull your victim's arm out straight toward you, still twisting, and fall back to position on your back. Your victim's elbow and wrist will be broken.

**No. 486. Trick 50. Phase 1**

Should your opponent throw his right arm around your neck, and his left arm around your waist, swing suddenly and forcibly around to your own right. This breaks the hold that your adversary has taken with his left arm and leaves him with his right arm around your neck. With both of your hands instantly seize his right hand and bend forward, and you are ready to throw your opponent by the trick known to American wrestlers as the " flying mare." Of course, your antagonist resists the throw by pulling backward, and, as he does so, your surest defence is to drop quickly to your right knee at his side, flexing his captured right hand over upon his wrist. Now you are able to rise behind him, still flexing your opponent's captured hand with your left hand. At the same time throw your right arm back of his neck, around at the left side of his neck, and seize his right lapel. Press your right knee against the outside of your antagonist's right knee, and pitch him forward to the position shown in illustration No. 486.

**No. 487. Trick 50. Phase 2**

In the last phase, by pulling hard on your opponent's captured lapel, you were able to choke him into submission. If, on the other hand, you preferred to make him touch on both shoulders, then, having retained your original hold on his captured right hand, pull your victim over to his left, making him touch his shoulders to the ground.

A CATALOGUE OF SELECTED DOVER BOOKS
IN ALL FIELDS OF INTEREST

# A CATALOGUE OF SELECTED DOVER BOOKS
# IN ALL FIELDS OF INTEREST

AMERICA'S OLD MASTERS, James T. Flexner. Four men emerged unexpectedly from provincial 18th century America to leadership in European art: Benjamin West, J. S. Copley, C. R. Peale, Gilbert Stuart. Brilliant coverage of lives and contributions. Revised, 1967 edition. 69 plates. 365pp. of text.

21806-6 Paperbound $3.00

FIRST FLOWERS OF OUR WILDERNESS: AMERICAN PAINTING, THE COLONIAL PERIOD, James T. Flexner. Painters, and regional painting traditions from earliest Colonial times up to the emergence of Copley, West and Peale Sr., Foster, Gustavus Hesselius, Feke, John Smibert and many anonymous painters in the primitive manner. Engaging presentation, with 162 illustrations. xxii + 368pp.

22180-6 Paperbound $3.50

THE LIGHT OF DISTANT SKIES: AMERICAN PAINTING, 1760-1835, James T. Flexner. The great generation of early American painters goes to Europe to learn and to teach: West, Copley, Gilbert Stuart and others. Allston, Trumbull, Morse; also contemporary American painters—primitives, derivatives, academics—who remained in America. 102 illustrations. xiii + 306pp. 22179-2 Paperbound $3.50

A HISTORY OF THE RISE AND PROGRESS OF THE ARTS OF DESIGN IN THE UNITED STATES, William Dunlap. Much the richest mine of information on early American painters, sculptors, architects, engravers, miniaturists, etc. The only source of information for scores of artists, the major primary source for many others. Unabridged reprint of rare original 1834 edition, with new introduction by James T. Flexner, and 394 new illustrations. Edited by Rita Weiss. 6⅝ x 9⅝.

21695-0, 21696-9, 21697-7 Three volumes, Paperbound $15.00

EPOCHS OF CHINESE AND JAPANESE ART, Ernest F. Fenollosa. From primitive Chinese art to the 20th century, thorough history, explanation of every important art period and form, including Japanese woodcuts; main stress on China and Japan, but Tibet, Korea also included. Still unexcelled for its detailed, rich coverage of cultural background, aesthetic elements, diffusion studies, particularly of the historical period. 2nd, 1913 edition. 242 illustrations. lii + 439pp. of text.

20364-6, 20365-4 Two volumes, Paperbound $6.00

THE GENTLE ART OF MAKING ENEMIES, James A. M. Whistler. Greatest wit of his day deflates Oscar Wilde, Ruskin, Swinburne; strikes back at inane critics, exhibitions, art journalism; aesthetics of impressionist revolution in most striking form. Highly readable classic by great painter. Reproduction of edition designed by Whistler. Introduction by Alfred Werner. xxxvi + 334pp.

21875-9 Paperbound $3.00

VISUAL ILLUSIONS: THEIR CAUSES, CHARACTERISTICS, AND APPLICATIONS, Matthew Luckiesh. Thorough description and discussion of optical illusion, geometric and perspective, particularly; size and shape distortions, illusions of color, of motion; natural illusions; use of illusion in art and magic, industry, etc. Most useful today with op art, also for classical art. Scores of effects illustrated. Introduction by William H. Ittleson. 100 illustrations. xxi + 252pp.

21530-X Paperbound $2.00

A HANDBOOK OF ANATOMY FOR ART STUDENTS, Arthur Thomson. Thorough, virtually exhaustive coverage of skeletal structure, musculature, etc. Full text, supplemented by anatomical diagrams and drawings and by photographs of undraped figures. Unique in its comparison of male and female forms, pointing out differences of contour, texture, form. 211 figures, 40 drawings, 86 photographs. xx + 459pp. 5⅜ x 8⅜.

21163-0 Paperbound $3.50

150 MASTERPIECES OF DRAWING, Selected by Anthony Toney. Full page reproductions of drawings from the early 16th to the end of the 18th century, all beautifully reproduced: Rembrandt, Michelangelo, Dürer, Fragonard, Urs, Graf, Wouwerman, many others. First-rate browsing book, model book for artists. xviii + 150pp. 8⅜ x 11¼.

21032-4 Paperbound· $3.50

THE LATER WORK OF AUBREY BEARDSLEY, Aubrey Beardsley. Exotic, erotic, ironic masterpieces in full maturity: Comedy Ballet, Venus and Tannhauser, Pierrot, Lysistrata, Rape of the Lock, Savoy material, Ali Baba, Volpone, etc. This material revolutionized the art world, and is still powerful, fresh, brilliant. With *The Early Work,* all Beardsley's finest work. 174 plates, 2 in color. xiv + 176pp. 8⅛ x 11.

21817-1 Paperbound $3.75

DRAWINGS OF REMBRANDT, Rembrandt van Rijn. Complete reproduction of fabulously rare edition by Lippmann and Hofstede de Groot, completely reedited, updated, improved by Prof. Seymour Slive, Fogg Museum. Portraits, Biblical sketches, landscapes, Oriental types, nudes, episodes from classical mythology—All Rembrandt's fertile genius. Also selection of drawings by his pupils and followers. "Stunning volumes," *Saturday Review.* 550 illustrations. lxxviii + 552pp. 9⅛ x 12¼.

21485-0, 21486-9 Two volumes, Paperbound $10.00

THE DISASTERS OF WAR, Francisco Goya. One of the masterpieces of Western civilization—83 etchings that record Goya's shattering, bitter reaction to the Napoleonic war that swept through Spain after the insurrection of 1808 and to war in general. Reprint of the first edition, with three additional plates from Boston's Museum of Fine Arts. All plates facsimile size. Introduction by Philip Hofer, Fogg Museum. v + 97pp. 9⅜ x 8¼.

21872-4 Paperbound $2.50

GRAPHIC WORKS OF ODILON REDON. Largest collection of Redon's graphic works ever assembled: 172 lithographs, 28 etchings and engravings, 9 drawings. These include some of his most famous works. All the plates from *Odilon Redon: oeuvre graphique complet,* plus additional plates. New introduction and caption translations by Alfred Werner. 209 illustrations. xxvii + 209pp. 9⅛ x 12¼.

21966-8 Paperbound $5.00

DESIGN BY ACCIDENT; A BOOK OF "ACCIDENTAL EFFECTS" FOR ARTISTS AND DESIGNERS, James F. O'Brien. Create your own unique, striking, imaginative effects by "controlled accident" interaction of materials: paints and lacquers, oil and water based paints, splatter, crackling materials, shatter, similar items. Everything you do will be different; first book on this limitless art, so useful to both fine artist and commercial artist. Full instructions. 192 plates showing "accidents," 8 in color. viii + 215pp. 8⅜ x 11¼.                                   21942-9 Paperbound $3.75

THE BOOK OF SIGNS, Rudolf Koch. Famed German type designer draws 493 beautiful symbols: religious, mystical, alchemical, imperial, property marks, runes, etc. Remarkable fusion of traditional and modern. Good for suggestions of timelessness, smartness, modernity. Text. vi + 104pp. 6⅛ x 9¼.
                                                          20162-7 Paperbound $1.25

HISTORY OF INDIAN AND INDONESIAN ART, Ananda K. Coomaraswamy. An unabridged republication of one of the finest books by a great scholar in Eastern art. Rich in descriptive material, history, social backgrounds; Sunga reliefs, Rajput paintings, Gupta temples, Burmese frescoes, textiles, jewelry, sculpture, etc. 400 photos. viii + 423pp. 6⅜ x 9¾.                     21436-2 Paperbound $5.00

PRIMITIVE ART, Franz Boas. America's foremost anthropologist surveys textiles, ceramics, woodcarving, basketry, metalwork, etc.; patterns, technology, creation of symbols, style origins. All areas of world, but very full on Northwest Coast Indians. More than 350 illustrations of baskets, boxes, totem poles, weapons, etc. 378 pp.
                                                          20025-6 Paperbound $3.00

THE GENTLEMAN AND CABINET MAKER'S DIRECTOR, Thomas Chippendale. Full reprint (third edition, 1762) of most influential furniture book of all time, by master cabinetmaker. 200 plates, illustrating chairs, sofas, mirrors, tables, cabinets, plus 24 photographs of surviving pieces. Biographical introduction by N. Bienenstock. vi + 249pp. 9⅞ x 12¾.                     21601-2 Paperbound $4.00

AMERICAN ANTIQUE FURNITURE, Edgar G. Miller, Jr. The basic coverage of all American furniture before 1840. Individual chapters cover type of furniture—clocks, tables, sideboards, etc.—chronologically, with inexhaustible wealth of data. More than 2100 photographs, all identified, commented on. Essential to all early American collectors. Introduction by H. E. Keyes. vi + 1106pp. 7⅞ x 10¾.
                            21599-7, 21600-4 Two volumes, Paperbound $11.00

PENNSYLVANIA DUTCH AMERICAN FOLK ART, Henry J. Kauffman. 279 photos, 28 drawings of tulipware, Fraktur script, painted tinware, toys, flowered furniture, quilts, samplers, hex signs, house interiors, etc. Full descriptive text. Excellent for tourist, rewarding for designer, collector. Map. 146pp. 7⅞ x 10¾.
                                                          21205-X Paperbound $2.50

EARLY NEW ENGLAND GRAVESTONE RUBBINGS, Edmund V. Gillon, Jr. 43 photographs, 226 carefully reproduced rubbings show heavily symbolic, sometimes macabre early gravestones, up to early 19th century. Remarkable early American primitive art, occasionally strikingly beautiful; always powerful. Text. xxvi + 207pp. 8⅜ x 11¼.                                   21380-3 Paperbound $3.50

ALPHABETS AND ORNAMENTS, Ernst Lehner. Well-known pictorial source for decorative alphabets, script examples, cartouches, frames, decorative title pages, calligraphic initials, borders, similar material. 14th to 19th century, mostly European. Useful in almost any graphic arts designing, varied styles. 750 illustrations. 256pp. 7 x 10. 21905-4 Paperbound $4.00

PAINTING: A CREATIVE APPROACH, Norman Colquhoun. For the beginner simple guide provides an instructive approach to painting: major stumbling blocks for beginner; overcoming them, technical points; paints and pigments; oil painting; watercolor and other media and color. New section on "plastic" paints. Glossary. Formerly *Paint Your Own Pictures*. 221pp. 22000-1 Paperbound $1.75

THE ENJOYMENT AND USE OF COLOR, Walter Sargent. Explanation of the relations between colors themselves and between colors in nature and art, including hundreds of little-known facts about color values, intensities, effects of high and low illumination, complementary colors. Many practical hints for painters, references to great masters. 7 color plates, 29 illustrations. x + 274pp. 20944-X Paperbound $2.75

THE NOTEBOOKS OF LEONARDO DA VINCI, compiled and edited by Jean Paul Richter. 1566 extracts from original manuscripts reveal the full range of Leonardo's versatile genius: all his writings on painting, sculpture, architecture, anatomy, astronomy, geography, topography, physiology, mining, music, etc., in both Italian and English, with 186 plates of manuscript pages and more than 500 additional drawings. Includes studies for the Last Supper, the lost Sforza monument, and other works. Total of xlvii + 866pp. 7⅞ x 10¾. 22572-0, 22573-9 Two volumes, Paperbound $11.00

MONTGOMERY WARD CATALOGUE OF 1895. Tea gowns, yards of flannel and pillow-case lace, stereoscopes, books of gospel hymns, the New Improved Singer Sewing Machine, side saddles, milk skimmers, straight-edged razors, high-button shoes, spittoons, and on and on ... listing some 25,000 items, practically all illustrated. Essential to the shoppers of the 1890's, it is our truest record of the spirit of the period. Unaltered reprint of Issue No. 57, Spring and Summer 1895. Introduction by Boris Emmet. Innumerable illustrations. xiii + 624pp. 8½ x 11⅝. 22377-9 Paperbound $6.95

THE CRYSTAL PALACE EXHIBITION ILLUSTRATED CATALOGUE (LONDON, 1851). One of the wonders of the modern world—the Crystal Palace Exhibition in which all the nations of the civilized world exhibited their achievements in the arts and sciences—presented in an equally important illustrated catalogue. More than 1700 items pictured with accompanying text—ceramics, textiles, cast-iron work, carpets, pianos, sleds, razors, wall-papers, billiard tables, beehives, silverware and hundreds of other artifacts represent the focal point of Victorian culture in the Western World. Probably the largest collection of Victorian decorative art ever assembled—indispensable for antiquarians and designers. Unabridged republication of the Art-Journal Catalogue of the Great Exhibition of 1851, with all terminal essays. New introduction by John Gloag, F.S.A. xxxiv + 426pp. 9 x 12. 22503-8 Paperbound $5.00

CATALOGUE OF DOVER BOOKS

A HISTORY OF COSTUME, Carl Köhler. Definitive history, based on surviving pieces of clothing primarily, and paintings, statues, etc. secondarily. Highly readable text, supplemented by 594 illustrations of costumes of the ancient Mediterranean peoples, Greece and Rome, the Teutonic prehistoric period; costumes of the Middle Ages, Renaissance, Baroque, 18th and 19th centuries. Clear, measured patterns are provided for many clothing articles. Approach is practical throughout. Enlarged by Emma von Sichart. 464pp. 21030-8 Paperbound $3.50.

ORIENTAL RUGS, ANTIQUE AND MODERN, Walter A. Hawley. A complete and authoritative treatise on the Oriental rug—where they are made, by whom and how, designs and symbols, characteristics in detail of the six major groups, how to distinguish them and how to buy them. Detailed technical data is provided on periods, weaves, warps, wefts, textures, sides, ends and knots, although no technical background is required for an understanding. 11 color plates, 80 halftones, 4 maps. vi + 320pp. 6⅛ x 9⅛. 22366-3 Paperbound $5.00

TEN BOOKS ON ARCHITECTURE, Vitruvius. By any standards the most important book on architecture ever written. Early Roman discussion of aesthetics of building, construction methods, orders, sites, and every other aspect of architecture has inspired, instructed architecture for about 2,000 years. Stands behind Palladio, Michelangelo, Bramante, Wren, countless others. Definitive Morris H. Morgan translation. 68 illustrations. xii + 331pp. 20645-9 Paperbound $3.00

THE FOUR BOOKS OF ARCHITECTURE, Andrea Palladio. Translated into every major Western European language in the two centuries following its publication in 1570, this has been one of the most influential books in the history of architecture. Complete reprint of the 1738 Isaac Ware edition. New introduction by Adolf Placzek, Columbia Univ. 216 plates. xxii + 110pp. of text. 9½ x 12¾. 21308-0 Clothbound $12.50

STICKS AND STONES: A STUDY OF AMERICAN ARCHITECTURE AND CIVILIZATION, Lewis Mumford.One of the great classics of American cultural history. American architecture from the medieval-inspired earliest forms to the early 20th century; evolution of structure and style, and reciprocal influences on environment. 21 photographic illustrations. 238pp. 20202-X Paperbound $2.00

THE AMERICAN BUILDER'S COMPANION, Asher Benjamin. The most widely used early 19th century architectural style and source book, for colonial up into Greek Revival periods. Extensive development of geometry of carpentering, construction of sashes, frames, doors, stairs; plans and elevations of domestic and other buildings. Hundreds of thousands of houses were built according to this book, now invaluable to historians, architects, restorers, etc. 1827 edition. 59 plates. 114pp. 7⅞ x 10¾. 22236-5 Paperbound $3.50

DUTCH HOUSES IN THE HUDSON VALLEY BEFORE 1776, Helen Wilkinson Reynolds. The standard survey of the Dutch colonial house and outbuildings, with constructional features, decoration, and local history associated with individual homesteads. Introduction by Franklin D. Roosevelt. Map. 150 illustrations. 469pp. 6⅝ x 9¼. 21469-9 Paperbound $5.00

THE ARCHITECTURE OF COUNTRY HOUSES, Andrew J. Downing. Together with Vaux's *Villas and Cottages* this is the basic book for Hudson River Gothic architecture of the middle Victorian period. Full, sound discussions of general aspects of housing, architecture, style, decoration, furnishing, together with scores of detailed house plans, illustrations of specific buildings, accompanied by full text. Perhaps the most influential single American architectural book. 1850 edition. Introduction by J. Stewart Johnson. 321 figures, 34 architectural designs. xvi + 560pp.
22003-6 Paperbound $4.00

LOST EXAMPLES OF COLONIAL ARCHITECTURE, John Mead Howells. Full-page photographs of buildings that have disappeared or been so altered as to be denatured, including many designed by major early American architects. 245 plates. xvii + 248pp. 7⅞ x 10¾. 21143-6 Paperbound $3.50

DOMESTIC ARCHITECTURE OF THE AMERICAN COLONIES AND OF THE EARLY REPUBLIC, Fiske Kimball. Foremost architect and restorer of Williamsburg and Monticello covers nearly 200 homes between 1620-1825. Architectural details, construction, style features, special fixtures, floor plans, etc. Generally considered finest work in its area. 219 illustrations of houses, doorways, windows, capital mantels. xx + 314pp. 7⅞ x 10¾. 21743-4 Paperbound $4.00

EARLY AMERICAN ROOMS: 1650-1858, edited by Russell Hawes Kettell. Tour of 12 rooms, each representative of a different era in American history and each furnished, decorated, designed and occupied in the style of the era. 72 plans and elevations, 8-page color section, etc., show fabrics, wall papers, arrangements, etc. Full descriptive text. xvii + 200pp. of text. 8⅜ x 11¼. 21633-0 Paperbound $5.00

THE FITZWILLIAM VIRGINAL BOOK, edited by J. Fuller Maitland and W. B. Squire. Full modern printing of famous early 17th-century ms. volume of 300 works by Morley, Byrd, Bull, Gibbons, etc. For piano or other modern keyboard instrument; easy to read format. xxxvi + 938pp. 8⅜ x 11. 21068-5, 21069-3 Two volumes, Paperbound$10.00

KEYBOARD MUSIC, Johann Sebastian Bach. Bach Gesellschaft edition. A rich selection of Bach's masterpieces for the harpsichord: the six English Suites, six French Suites, the six Partitas (Clavierübung part I), the Goldberg Variations (Clavierübung part IV), the fifteen Two-Part Inventions and the fifteen Three-Part Sinfonias. Clearly reproduced on large sheets with ample margins; eminently playable. vi + 312pp. 8⅛ x 11. 22360-4 Paperbound $5.00

THE MUSIC OF BACH: AN INTRODUCTION, Charles Sanford Terry. A fine, nontechnical introduction to Bach's music, both instrumental and vocal. Covers organ music, chamber music, passion music, other types. Analyzes themes, developments, innovations. x + 114pp. 21075-8 Paperbound $1.50

BEETHOVEN AND HIS NINE SYMPHONIES, Sir George Grove. Noted British musicologist provides best history, analysis, commentary on symphonies. Very thorough, rigorously accurate; necessary to both advanced student and amateur music lover. 436 musical passages. vii + 407 pp. 20334-4 Paperbound $2.75

JOHANN SEBASTIAN BACH, Philipp Spitta. One of the great classics of musicology, this definitive analysis of Bach's music (and life) has never been surpassed. Lucid, nontechnical analyses of hundreds of pieces (30 pages devoted to St. Matthew Passion, 26 to B Minor Mass). Also includes major analysis of 18th-century music. 450 musical examples. 40-page musical supplement. Total of xx + 1799pp.
(EUK) 22278-0, 22279-9 Two volumes, Clothbound $17.50

MOZART AND HIS PIANO CONCERTOS, Cuthbert Girdlestone. The only full-length study of an important area of Mozart's creativity. Provides detailed analyses of all 23 concertos, traces inspirational sources. 417 musical examples. Second edition. 509pp. 21271-8 Paperbound $3.50

THE PERFECT WAGNERITE: A COMMENTARY ON THE NIBLUNG'S RING, George Bernard Shaw. Brilliant and still relevant criticism in remarkable essays on Wagner's Ring cycle, Shaw's ideas on political and social ideology behind the plots, role of Leitmotifs, vocal requisites, etc. Prefaces. xxi + 136pp.
(USO) 21707-8 Paperbound $1.75

DON GIOVANNI, W. A. Mozart. Complete libretto, modern English translation; biographies of composer and librettist; accounts of early performances and critical reaction. Lavishly illustrated. All the material you need to understand and appreciate this great work. Dover Opera Guide and Libretto Series; translated and introduced by Ellen Bleiler. 92 illustrations. 209pp.
21134-7 Paperbound $2.00

BASIC ELECTRICITY, U. S. Bureau of Naval Personel. Originally a training course, best non-technical coverage of basic theory of electricity and its applications. Fundamental concepts, batteries, circuits, conductors and wiring techniques, AC and DC, inductance and capacitance, generators, motors, transformers, magnetic amplifiers, synchros, servomechanisms, etc. Also covers blue-prints, electrical diagrams, etc. Many questions, with answers. 349 illustrations. x + 448pp. 6½ x 9¼.
20973-3 Paperbound $3.50

REPRODUCTION OF SOUND, Edgar Villchur. Thorough coverage for laymen of high fidelity systems, reproducing systems in general, needles, amplifiers, preamps, loudspeakers, feedback, explaining physical background. "A rare talent for making technicalities vividly comprehensible," R. Darrell, *High Fidelity*. 69 figures. iv + 92pp. 21515-6 Paperbound $1.35

HEAR ME TALKIN' TO YA: THE STORY OF JAZZ AS TOLD BY THE MEN WHO MADE IT, Nat Shapiro and Nat Hentoff. Louis Armstrong, Fats Waller, Jo Jones, Clarence Williams, Billy Holiday, Duke Ellington, Jelly Roll Morton and dozens of other jazz greats tell how it was in Chicago's South Side, New Orleans, depression Harlem and the modern West Coast as jazz was born and grew. xvi + 429pp.
21726-4 Paperbound $3.00

FABLES OF AESOP, translated by Sir Roger L'Estrange. A reproduction of the very rare 1931 Paris edition; a selection of the most interesting fables, together with 50 imaginative drawings by Alexander Calder. v + 128pp. 6½x9¼.
21780-9 Paperbound $1.50

AGAINST THE GRAIN (A REBOURS), Joris K. Huysmans. Filled with weird images, evidences of a bizarre imagination, exotic experiments with hallucinatory drugs, rich tastes and smells and the diversions of its sybarite hero Duc Jean des Esseintes, this classic novel pushed 19th-century literary decadence to its limits. Full unabridged edition. Do not confuse this with abridged editions generally sold. Introduction by Havelock Ellis. xlix + 206pp.                     22190-3 Paperbound $2.50

VARIORUM SHAKESPEARE: HAMLET. Edited by Horace H. Furness; a landmark of American scholarship. Exhaustive footnotes and appendices treat all doubtful words and phrases, as well as suggested critical emendations throughout the play's history. First volume contains editor's own text, collated with all Quartos and Folios. Second volume contains full first Quarto, translations of Shakespeare's sources (Belleforest, and Saxo Grammaticus), Der Bestrafte Brudermord, and many essays on critical and historical points of interest by major authorities of past and present. Includes details of staging and costuming over the years. By far the best edition available for serious students of Shakespeare. Total of xx + 905pp.
21004-9, 21005-7, 2 volumes, Paperbound $7.00

A LIFE OF WILLIAM SHAKESPEARE, Sir Sidney Lee. This is the standard life of Shakespeare, summarizing everything known about Shakespeare and his plays. Incredibly rich in material, broad in coverage, clear and judicious, it has served thousands as the best introduction to Shakespeare. 1931 edition. 9 plates. xxix + 792pp.                     21967-4 Paperbound $4.50

MASTERS OF THE DRAMA, John Gassner. Most comprehensive history of the drama in print, covering every tradition from Greeks to modern Europe and America, including India, Far East, etc. Covers more than 800 dramatists, 2000 plays, with biographical material, plot summaries, theatre history, criticism, etc. "Best of its kind in English," New Republic. 77 illustrations. xxii + 890pp.
20100-7 Clothbound $10.00

THE EVOLUTION OF THE ENGLISH LANGUAGE, George McKnight. The growth of English, from the 14th century to the present. Unusual, non-technical account presents basic information in very interesting form: sound shifts, change in grammar and syntax, vocabulary growth, similar topics. Abundantly illustrated with quotations. Formerly Modern English in the Making. xii + 590pp.
21932-1 Paperbound $4.00

AN ETYMOLOGICAL DICTIONARY OF MODERN ENGLISH, Ernest Weekley. Fullest, richest work of its sort, by foremost British lexicographer. Detailed word histories, including many colloquial and archaic words; extensive quotations. Do not confuse this with the Concise Etymological Dictionary, which is much abridged. Total of xxvii + 830pp. 6½ x 9¼.
21873-2, 21874-0 Two volumes, Paperbound $7.90

FLATLAND: A ROMANCE OF MANY DIMENSIONS, E. A. Abbott. Classic of science-fiction explores ramifications of life in a two-dimensional world, and what happens when a three-dimensional being intrudes. Amusing reading, but also useful as introduction to thought about hyperspace. Introduction by Banesh Hoffmann. 16 illustrations. xx + 103pp.                     20001-9 Paperbound $1.25

POEMS OF ANNE BRADSTREET, edited with an introduction by Robert Hutchinson. A new selection of poems by America's first poet and perhaps the first significant woman poet in the English language. 48 poems display her development in works of considerable variety—love poems, domestic poems, religious meditations, formal elegies, "quaternions," etc. Notes, bibliography. viii + 222pp.
22160-1 Paperbound $2.50

THREE GOTHIC NOVELS: THE CASTLE OF OTRANTO BY HORACE WALPOLE; VATHEK BY WILLIAM BECKFORD; THE VAMPYRE BY JOHN POLIDORI, WITH FRAGMENT OF A NOVEL BY LORD BYRON, edited by E. F. Bleiler. The first Gothic novel, by Walpole; the finest Oriental tale in English, by Beckford; powerful Romantic supernatural story in versions by Polidori and Byron. All extremely important in history of literature; all still exciting, packed with supernatural thrills, ghosts, haunted castles, magic, etc. xl + 291pp.
21232-7 Paperbound $2.50

THE BEST TALES OF HOFFMANN, E. T. A. Hoffmann. 10 of Hoffmann's most important stories, in modern re-editings of standard translations: Nutcracker and the King of Mice, Signor Formica, Automata, The Sandman, Rath Krespel, The Golden Flowerpot, Master Martin the Cooper, The Mines of Falun, The King's Betrothed, A New Year's Eve Adventure. 7 illustrations by Hoffmann. Edited by E. F. Bleiler. xxxix + 419pp.
21793-0 Paperbound $3.00

GHOST AND HORROR STORIES OF AMBROSE BIERCE, Ambrose Bierce. 23 strikingly modern stories of the horrors latent in the human mind: The Eyes of the Panther, The Damned Thing, An Occurrence at Owl Creek Bridge, An Inhabitant of Carcosa, etc., plus the dream-essay, Visions of the Night. Edited by E. F. Bleiler. xxii + 199pp.
20767-6 Paperbound $1.50

BEST GHOST STORIES OF J. S. LEFANU, J. Sheridan LeFanu. Finest stories by Victorian master often considered greatest supernatural writer of all. Carmilla, Green Tea, The Haunted Baronet, The Familiar, and 12 others. Most never before available in the U. S. A. Edited by E. F. Bleiler. 8 illustrations from Victorian publications. xvii + 467pp.
20415-4 Paperbound $3.00

MATHEMATICAL FOUNDATIONS OF INFORMATION THEORY, A. I. Khinchin. Comprehensive introduction to work of Shannon, McMillan, Feinstein and Khinchin, placing these investigations on a rigorous mathematical basis. Covers entropy concept in probability theory, uniqueness theorem, Shannon's inequality, ergodic sources, the E property, martingale concept, noise, Feinstein's fundamental lemma, Shanon's first and second theorems. Translated by R. A. Silverman and M. D. Friedman. iii + 120pp.
60434-9 Paperbound $2.00

SEVEN SCIENCE FICTION NOVELS, H. G. Wells. The standard collection of the great novels. Complete, unabridged. *First Men in the Moon, Island of Dr. Moreau, War of the Worlds, Food of the Gods, Invisible Man, Time Machine, In the Days of the Comet.* Not only science fiction fans, but every educated person owes it to himself to read these novels. 1015pp.
(USO) 20264-X Clothbound $6.00

LAST AND FIRST MEN AND STAR MAKER, TWO SCIENCE FICTION NOVELS, Olaf Stapledon. Greatest future histories in science fiction. In the first, human intelligence is the "hero," through strange paths of evolution, interplanetary invasions, incredible technologies, near extinctions and reemergences. Star Maker describes the quest of a band of star rovers for intelligence itself, through time and space: weird inhuman civilizations, crustacean minds, symbiotic worlds, etc. Complete, unabridged. v + 438pp. (USO) 21962-3 Paperbound $2.50

THREE PROPHETIC NOVELS, H. G. WELLS. Stages of a consistently planned future for mankind. *When the Sleeper Wakes,* and *A Story of the Days to Come,* anticipate *Brave New World* and *1984,* in the 21st Century; *The Time Machine,* only complete version in print, shows farther future and the end of mankind. All show Wells's greatest gifts as storyteller and novelist. Edited by E. F. Bleiler. x + 335pp. (USO) 20605-X Paperbound $2.50

THE DEVIL'S DICTIONARY, Ambrose Bierce. America's own Oscar Wilde—Ambrose Bierce—offers his barbed iconoclastic wisdom in over 1,000 definitions hailed by H. L. Mencken as "some of the most gorgeous witticisms in the English language." 145pp. 20487-1 Paperbound $1.25

MAX AND MORITZ, Wilhelm Busch. Great children's classic, father of comic strip, of two bad boys, Max and Moritz. Also Ker and Plunk (Plisch und Plumm), Cat and Mouse, Deceitful Henry, Ice-Peter, The Boy and the Pipe, and five other pieces. Original German, with English translation. Edited by H. Arthur Klein; translations by various hands and H. Arthur Klein. vi + 216pp. 20181-3 Paperbound $2.00

PIGS IS PIGS AND OTHER FAVORITES, Ellis Parker Butler. The title story is one of the best humor short stories, as Mike Flannery obfuscates biology and English. Also included, That Pup of Murchison's, The Great American Pie Company, and Perkins of Portland. 14 illustrations. v + 109pp. 21532-6 Paperbound $1.25

THE PETERKIN PAPERS, Lucretia P. Hale. It takes genius to be as stupidly mad as the Peterkins, as they decide to become wise, celebrate the "Fourth," keep a cow, and otherwise strain the resources of the Lady from Philadelphia. Basic book of American humor. 153 illustrations. 219pp. 20794-3 Paperbound $2.00

PERRAULT'S FAIRY TALES, translated by A. E. Johnson and S. R. Littlewood, with 34 full-page illustrations by Gustave Doré. All the original Perrault stories—Cinderella, Sleeping Beauty, Bluebeard, Little Red Riding Hood, Puss in Boots, Tom Thumb, etc.—with their witty verse morals and the magnificent illustrations of Doré. One of the five or six great books of European fairy tales. viii + 117pp. 8⅛ x 11. 22311-6 Paperbound $2.00

OLD HUNGARIAN FAIRY TALES, Baroness Orczy. Favorites translated and adapted by author of the *Scarlet Pimpernel.* Eight fairy tales include "The Suitors of Princess Fire-Fly," "The Twin Hunchbacks," "Mr. Cuttlefish's Love Story," and "The Enchanted Cat." This little volume of magic and adventure will captivate children as it has for generations. 90 drawings by Montagu Barstow. 96pp. (USO) 22293-4 Paperbound $1.95

THE RED FAIRY BOOK, Andrew Lang. Lang's color fairy books have long been children's favorites. This volume includes Rapunzel, Jack and the Bean-stalk and 35 other stories, familiar and unfamiliar. 4 plates, 93 illustrations x + 367pp.
21673-X Paperbound $2.50

THE BLUE FAIRY BOOK, Andrew Lang. Lang's tales come from all countries and all times. Here are 37 tales from Grimm, the Arabian Nights, Greek Mythology, and other fascinating sources. 8 plates, 130 illustrations. xi + 390pp.
21437-0 Paperbound $2.75

HOUSEHOLD STORIES BY THE BROTHERS GRIMM. Classic English-language edition of the well-known tales — Rumpelstiltskin, Snow White, Hansel and Gretel, The Twelve Brothers, Faithful John, Rapunzel, Tom Thumb (52 stories in all). Translated into simple, straightforward English by Lucy Crane. Ornamented with head-pieces, vignettes, elaborate decorative initials and a dozen full-page illustrations by Walter Crane. x + 269pp.
21080-4 Paperbound **$2.00**

THE MERRY ADVENTURES OF ROBIN HOOD, Howard Pyle. The finest modern versions of the traditional ballads and tales about the great English outlaw. Howard Pyle's complete prose version, with every word, every illustration of the first edition. Do not confuse this facsimile of the original (1883) with modern editions that change text or illustrations. 23 plates plus many page decorations. xxii + 296pp.
22043-5 Paperbound $2.75

THE STORY OF KING ARTHUR AND HIS KNIGHTS, Howard Pyle. The finest children's version of the life of King Arthur; brilliantly retold by Pyle, with 48 of his most imaginative illustrations. xviii + 313pp. 6⅛ x 9¼.
21445-1 Paperbound $2.50

THE WONDERFUL WIZARD OF OZ, L. Frank Baum. America's finest children's book in facsimile of first edition with all Denslow illustrations in full color. The edition a child should have. Introduction by Martin Gardner. 23 color plates, scores of drawings. iv + 267pp.
20691-2 Paperbound $2.50

THE MARVELOUS LAND OF OZ, L. Frank Baum. The second Oz book, every bit as imaginative as the Wizard. The hero is a boy named Tip, but the Scarecrow and the Tin Woodman are back, as is the Oz magic. 16 color plates, 120 drawings by John R. Neill. 287pp.
20692-0 Paperbound $2.50

THE MAGICAL MONARCH OF MO, L. Frank Baum. Remarkable adventures in a land even stranger than Oz. The best of Baum's books not in the Oz series. 15 color plates and dozens of drawings by Frank Verbeck. xviii + 237pp.
21892-9 Paperbound $2.25

THE BAD CHILD'S BOOK OF BEASTS, MORE BEASTS FOR WORSE CHILDREN, A MORAL ALPHABET, Hilaire Belloc. Three complete humor classics in one volume. Be kind to the frog, and do not call him names . . . and 28 other whimsical animals. Familiar favorites and some not so well known. Illustrated by Basil Blackwell. 156pp.
(USO) 20749-8 Paperbound $1.50

EAST O' THE SUN AND WEST O' THE MOON, George W. Dasent. Considered the best of all translations of these Norwegian folk tales, this collection has been enjoyed by generations of children (and folklorists too). Includes True and Untrue, Why the Sea is Salt, East O' the Sun and West O' the Moon, Why the Bear is Stumpy-Tailed, Boots and the Troll, The Cock and the Hen, Rich Peter the Pedlar, and 52 more. The only edition with all 59 tales. 77 illustrations by Erik Werenskiold and Theodor Kittelsen. xv + 418pp. 22521-6 Paperbound $3.50

GOOPS AND HOW TO BE THEM, Gelett Burgess. Classic of tongue-in-cheek humor, masquerading as etiquette book. 87 verses, twice as many cartoons, show mischievous Goops as they demonstrate to children virtues of table manners, neatness, courtesy, etc. Favorite for generations. viii + 88pp. 6½ x 9¼. 22233-0 Paperbound $1.50

ALICE'S ADVENTURES UNDER GROUND, Lewis Carroll. The first version, quite different from the final *Alice in Wonderland,* printed out by Carroll himself with his own illustrations. Complete facsimile of the "million dollar" manuscript Carroll gave to Alice Liddell in 1864. Introduction by Martin Gardner. viii + 96pp. Title and dedication pages in color. 21482-6 Paperbound $1.25

THE BROWNIES, THEIR BOOK, Palmer Cox. Small as mice, cunning as foxes, exuberant and full of mischief, the Brownies go to the zoo, toy shop, seashore, circus, etc., in 24 verse adventures and 266 illustrations. Long a favorite, since their first appearance in St. Nicholas Magazine. xi + 144pp. 6⅝ x 9¼. 21265-3 Paperbound $1.75

SONGS OF CHILDHOOD, Walter De La Mare. Published (under the pseudonym Walter Ramal) when De La Mare was only 29, this charming collection has long been a favorite children's book. A facsimile of the first edition in paper, the 47 poems capture the simplicity of the nursery rhyme and the ballad, including such lyrics as I Met Eve, Tartary, The Silver Penny. vii + 106pp. (USO) 21972-0 Paperbound $2.00

THE COMPLETE NONSENSE OF EDWARD LEAR, Edward Lear. The finest 19th-century humorist-cartoonist in full: all nonsense limericks, zany alphabets, Owl and Pussycat, songs, nonsense botany, and more than 500 illustrations by Lear himself. Edited by Holbrook Jackson. xxix + 287pp. (USO) 20167-8 Paperbound $2.00

BILLY WHISKERS: THE AUTOBIOGRAPHY OF A GOAT, Frances Trego Montgomery. A favorite of children since the early 20th century, here are the escapades of that rambunctious, irresistible and mischievous goat—Billy Whiskers. Much in the spirit of *Peck's Bad Boy,* this is a book that children never tire of reading or hearing. All the original familiar illustrations by W. H. Fry are included: 6 color plates, 18 black and white drawings. 159pp. 22345-0 Paperbound $2.00

MOTHER GOOSE MELODIES. Faithful republication of the fabulously rare Munroe and Francis "copyright 1833" Boston edition—the most important Mother Goose collection, usually referred to as the "original." Familiar rhymes plus many rare ones, with wonderful old woodcut illustrations. Edited by E. F. Bleiler. 128pp. 4½ x 6⅜. 22577-1 Paperbound $1.00

TWO LITTLE SAVAGES; BEING THE ADVENTURES OF TWO BOYS WHO LIVED AS INDIANS AND WHAT THEY LEARNED, Ernest Thompson Seton. Great classic of nature and boyhood provides a vast range of woodlore in most palatable form, a genuinely entertaining story. Two farm boys build a teepee in woods and live in it for a month, working out Indian solutions to living problems, star lore, birds and animals, plants, etc. 293 illustrations. vii + 286pp.

20985-7 Paperbound $2.50

PETER PIPER'S PRACTICAL PRINCIPLES OF PLAIN & PERFECT PRONUNCIATION. Alliterative jingles and tongue-twisters of surprising charm, that made their first appearance in America about 1830. Republished in full with the spirited woodcut illustrations from this earliest American edition. 32pp. 4½ x 6⅜.

22560-7 Paperbound $1.00

SCIENCE EXPERIMENTS AND AMUSEMENTS FOR CHILDREN, Charles Vivian. 73 easy experiments, requiring only materials found at home or easily available, such as candles, coins, steel wool, etc.; illustrate basic phenomena like vacuum, simple chemical reaction, etc. All safe. Modern, well-planned. Formerly *Science Games for Children*. 102 photos, numerous drawings. 96pp. 6⅛ x 9¼.

21856-2 Paperbound $1.25

AN INTRODUCTION TO CHESS MOVES AND TACTICS SIMPLY EXPLAINED, Leonard Barden. Informal intermediate introduction, quite strong in explaining reasons for moves. Covers basic material, tactics, important openings, traps, positional play in middle game, end game. Attempts to isolate patterns and recurrent configurations. Formerly *Chess*. 58 figures. 102pp. (USO) 21210-6 Paperbound $1.25

LASKER'S MANUAL OF CHESS, Dr. Emanuel Lasker. Lasker was not only one of the five great World Champions, he was also one of the ablest expositors, theorists, and analysts. In many ways, his Manual, permeated with his philosophy of battle, filled with keen insights, is one of the greatest works ever written on chess. Filled with analyzed games by the great players. A single-volume library that will profit almost any chess player, beginner or master. 308 diagrams. xli x 349pp.

20640-8 Paperbound $2.75

THE MASTER BOOK OF MATHEMATICAL RECREATIONS, Fred Schuh. In opinion of many the finest work ever prepared on mathematical puzzles, stunts, recreations; exhaustively thorough explanations of mathematics involved, analysis of effects, citation of puzzles and games. Mathematics involved is elementary. Translated by F. Göbel. 194 figures. xxiv + 430pp. 22134-2 Paperbound $3.50

MATHEMATICS, MAGIC AND MYSTERY, Martin Gardner. Puzzle editor for Scientific American explains mathematics behind various mystifying tricks: card tricks, stage "mind reading," coin and match tricks, counting out games, geometric dissections, etc. Probability sets, theory of numbers clearly explained. Also provides more than 400 tricks, guaranteed to work, that you can do. 135 illustrations. xii + 176pp.

20335-2 Paperbound $1.75

MATHEMATICAL PUZZLES FOR BEGINNERS AND ENTHUSIASTS, Geoffrey Mott-Smith. 189 puzzles from easy to difficult—involving arithmetic, logic, algebra, properties of digits, probability, etc.—for enjoyment and mental stimulus. Explanation of mathematical principles behind the puzzles. 135 illustrations. viii + 248pp.
20198-8 Paperbound $1.75

PAPER FOLDING FOR BEGINNERS, William D. Murray and Francis J. Rigney. Easiest book on the market, clearest instructions on making interesting, beautiful origami. Sail boats, cups, roosters, frogs that move legs, bonbon boxes, standing birds, etc. 40 projects; more than 275 diagrams and photographs. 94pp.
20713-7 Paperbound $1.00

TRICKS AND GAMES ON THE POOL TABLE, Fred Herrmann. 79 tricks and games— some solitaires, some for two or more players, some competitive games—to entertain you between formal games. Mystifying shots and throws, unusual caroms, tricks involving such props as cork, coins, a hat, etc. Formerly *Fun on the Pool Table*. 77 figures. 95pp.
21814-7 Paperbound $1.25

HAND SHADOWS TO BE THROWN UPON THE WALL: A SERIES OF NOVEL AND AMUSING FIGURES FORMED BY THE HAND, Henry Bursill. Delightful picturebook from great-grandfather's day shows how to make 18 different hand shadows: a bird that flies, duck that quacks, dog that wags his tail, camel, goose, deer, boy, turtle, etc. Only book of its sort. vi + 33pp. $6\frac{1}{2}$ x $9\frac{1}{4}$.
21779-5 Paperbound $1.00

WHITTLING AND WOODCARVING, E. J. Tangerman. 18th printing of best book on market. "If you can cut a potato you can carve" toys and puzzles, chains, chessmen, caricatures, masks, frames, woodcut blocks, surface patterns, much more. Information on tools, woods, techniques. Also goes into serious wood sculpture from Middle Ages to present, East and West. 464 photos, figures. x + 293pp.
20965-2 Paperbound $2.00

HISTORY OF PHILOSOPHY, Julián Marías. Possibly the clearest, most easily followed, best planned, most useful one-volume history of philosophy on the market; neither skimpy nor overfull. Full details on system of every major philosopher and dozens of less important thinkers from pre-Socratics up to Existentialism and later. Strong on many European figures usually omitted. Has gone through dozens of editions in Europe. 1966 edition, translated by Stanley Appelbaum and Clarence Strowbridge. xviii + 505pp.
21739-6 Paperbound $3.50

YOGA: A SCIENTIFIC EVALUATION, Kovoor T. Behanan. Scientific but non-technical study of physiological results of yoga exercises; done under auspices of Yale U. Relations to Indian thought, to psychoanalysis, etc. 16 photos. xxiii + 270pp.
20505-3 Paperbound $2.50

*Prices subject to change without notice.*
Available at your book dealer or write for free catalogue to Dept. GI, Dover Publications, Inc., 180 Varick St., N. Y., N. Y. 10014. Dover publishes more than 150 books each year on science, elementary and advanced mathematics, biology, music, art, literary history, social sciences and other areas.